EMPOWERED

FUTURE VOICES

Edited By Briony Kearney

First published in Great Britain in 2022 by:

Young Writers
Remus House
Coltsfoot Drive
Peterborough
PE2 9BF
Telephone: 01733 890066
Website: www.youngwriters.co.uk

Book Design by Ashley Janson

Softback ISBN 978-1-80015-852-8

Printed and bound in the UK by BookPrintingUK
Website: www.bookprintinguk.com
YB0498Q

FOREWORD

Since 1991, here at Young Writers we have celebrated the awesome power of creative writing, especially in young adults where it can serve as a vital method of expressing their emotions and views about the world around them. In every poem we see the effort and thought that each student published in this book has put into their work and by creating this anthology we hope to encourage them further with the ultimate goal of sparking a life-long love of writing.

Our latest competition for secondary school students, Empowered, challenged young writers to consider what was important to them. We wanted to give them a voice, the chance to express themselves freely and honestly, something which is so important for these young adults to feel confident and listened to. They could give an opinion, share a memory, consider a dilemma, impart advice or simply write about something they love. There were no restrictions on style or subject so you will find an anthology brimming with a variety of poetic styles and topics. We hope you find it as absorbing as we have.

We encourage young writers to express themselves and address subjects that matter to them, which sometimes means writing about sensitive or contentious topics. If you have been affected by any issues raised in this book, details on where to find help can be found at www.youngwriters.co.uk/info/other/contact-lines

☆ CONTENTS ☆

THE POEMS

Growing Old

It's quite a scary idea, to grow old by yourself,
People long for someone to hold, someone to help,
You need a friend through your highs and lows,
Someone kind, whose hand you can hold,
You won't win every competition or nail every test,
But beside someone you love, you'll feel at your best,
We'll start to crumble and fall into pieces,
But our chance of survival only increases,
"What doesn't kill you makes you stronger,"
It only makes you last a bit longer,
When we're young we think our time is limitless,
We'd think our whole life would be bliss,
But maturing isn't finding the meaning, however shocking,
Or even seeing Mum and Dad fill up your stocking,
It's taking it the hard way, learning to deal with it,
Managing challenges along the way, bit by bit,
Having a job, marriage, growing a family tree,
All those challenges are still ahead of me,
Then one day, the challenge will stop,
Our steady heartbeat will slowly drop,
When that time arrives, it won't be a fright,
We'll have that someone to hold, right?

Ruby-Rose Hamilton (12)

Dogs

I'm locked out of the house,
And I have no keys.
Nobody's home but light shines from a window.
Whilst I'm pounding away at the door,
The dog's howling on the other side,
And it is a genuine pity she is not physically capable
Of unlocking the door herself.

It's late. Really late,
And very cold.
I knock on the neighbour's door,
In the hopes of finding the spare key.
I tap, I knock,
But there is no answer.

Well,
I'll guess I'll walk to Grandma's,
It's okay, she lives five minutes away,
Just up the hill,
I've walked to her house a hundred times,
I'll go to Grandma's.

So off I set,
With no coat on and a dead phone,
In a white shirt and a dead phone,

Maybe I could take the shortcut,
But the shortcut is an alleyway,
And I'm not stupid.
I may be lazy but I'm not stupid.

Okay, I'll walk the long way,
Pass the corner shop and the laundrette,
Alongside the main road,
Which is busy for a 9 o'clock Sunday evening,
And pass the six bus stops we seem to so desperately need in this area,
(One outside Lidl... one opposite Lidl... one across the roundabout from Lidl... one across from the one across the roundabout from Lidl...)

I can't escape going up this one alleyway though,
Not technically an alley, more of a narrow road,
That is cornered off from the world,
It's a road that goes to the top of the hill,
Where my grandma lives,
But it's okay,
I've walked up this road loads of times,
And there are houses all along the side so,
Nothing too bad could happen.
Nothing too bad.

It's dark and besides the soft glow,
Of light coming from a few hours,
There are only two pathetic street lamps lighting

The way.
I walk.
Halfway up the hill,
I just seem to instinctively look behind me,
And nothing and no one's there,

Okay,
This is okay,
It's actually kind of enjoyable,
I see the appeal of late-night walks.

I'm three-quarters of the way up the hill,
And I look back again,
Instinctively,
My heart drops.
They've come out of nowhere,
Their face obscured by their large fur hood,
Their hands in their pockets,
Their feet steadily walking up the same hill as me.

I turn back around,
I think,
To what I've been taught,
From what I've learned.

Don't run.
Run and they know that you know
They are there.
It's most likely they'll chase after you,

And let's be honest,
I'm no Usain, there is no way,
I'm sprinting up the rest of this hill,
Don't look back,
They'll know you're onto them,

Instead, pick up your pace,
And don't seem panicked,
Pick up the phone,
Call someone, show them somebody will know
That you've gone missing,

But my phone's flat,
Lucky me.

So instead I pick up my pace,
And once I've reached the top of the hill,
And turn the corner,
I sprint for it.
I run down the main road,
So in case they catch up,
Maybe a car can come along and hit them,
So in case they catch up,
So in case I'm one of the unlucky ones,
I might be able to be found in the middle of a road,
Instead of the middle of a back alley.

I run, run, run,
This time looking back as I do,
Making sure they don't catch up,
Making sure I don't end up,
The next Sarah or Nessa.

I finally make it to my gran's door,
And I knock,
Not quite sure how to feel,
Glad or scared?

My mum opens the door,
And it turns out she's been there all the time,
I tell her
About the person in the alley.
"Well," she says, "you should have charged your phone."
My heart sinks.
"I should have charged my phone."
I should have charged my phone,
I should have had my keys,
I should have worn bright clothes,
I shouldn't have walked down that alley,
I shouldn't have got home so late,

I shouldn't have been born a girl.

Fifteen years later and I no longer like being a girl,
I no longer like sitting on the train,
Or the bus, or in the back of a taxi,

I no longer like wearing skirts,
I no longer like going out in public,
I no longer like staying out late,
I no longer like being alone,
I no longer like men,

The way they whistle at you like a dog,
The way they stare at you like a dog,
The way they expect you to sit there and obey,
And keep your temper whilst they pull your tail,
The way they see you like a dog,
Well, I might as well be a dog,
For a dog seems to have more rights than me,

But a dog has every right to snap back when being teased,
And I don't mind biting back,
Or being seen as a dog,
Because dogs are obedient,
Dogs are kind,
They are caring,
And because of this,
Men seem to underestimate that,
A pull too hard of a dog's tail,
Receives a brutal bite.

Mckenzie Spinks (15)

The Hatred You Inflict

A cknowledge Asia's existence! We shall not be treated without remorse!
S tereotypes thrown directly at our skulls like we were some targets in archery.
I deserve equality! Equality! We are all humans at the end of the day...
A dam and Eve also made a mistake however that does not define all of humanity
N ever! So why are Asians always inculpate in misinterpreted situations

A s helpless people collapse on the
C oncrete ground crying while drenched in blood, danger everywhere due to antagonists thinking they are far more superior than us
K illers on the loose. Hate crime and violence. Yet everyone is quiet
N o more! All of humankind should stand strong, solid and stoutly to end this menace
O pinions of righteous individuals are hated on and criticised
W hy are our distinctive attributes victimised
L unatics taking control but using my morals I'll speak up for those who can't and
E qual rights need to be given and more acknowledged
D anger pressurised on unimpeachable people and even adolescent children
G eneral talks produced into racial comment haunting us forever

E thical slurs drilled into adolescent children's minds
M y religion alludes my identity, culture, values, morals and that's a part of me
E thical backgrounds should be celebrated, adored, appreciated but instead there is
N ormalised racism when it comes to Asians' claimed as comedy, why?
T he word religion symbolises diversity and respect so stop the hate speech.

In my opinion, religion is a meaningful belief
And worship of a superior god.
This comes along with adequate teaching
For the individual which guides them through the right path.
So cease with the rumours and misconceptions.
Most significantly, no one should be judged
Due to their race or the colour of their skin,
Ethnicity, culture, religion.
We are all equal! Equal, I say,
So stop the segregation between humankind.

Shristi Kalyan (15)

Fitting In Is Addictive

Fitting in is addictive.
The sense of pride you feel,
From hiding yourself in a sea
Of normality and conscious stereotype.
It's the drug that fills
Every medicine cabinet.
Swarming originality under,
A blanket of empty minds
Descending into unified chaos.
A hive of subconscious breaths
Choking on thickened smoke.
Polluted air, tar in sluggish symphony,
Whipping the cobwebs of acceptance
Into a frenzy of forced conformity.
Repressed youths,
Fighting an endless battle
Against the bullets of ignorance,
That pummel in blind fear
Of the unknown and the abnormal.

Fitting in is addictive,
It wraps its arms around my neck
Fingers frail as glass,
But will as strong as steel
And as sharp as knives.
Slicing me down to fit the boxes

That I am unwillingly pushed into.
When a gentle nudge,
Turns to a push off a cliff.
Encasing my thoughts into a chest,
That hides in the depths of my mind,
Are keys lost in the ocean
That drowns my body
A sea of words, of fiction, of despair,
A jumble of my human anatomy
And fictive abnormality.
That strives to succumb me,
As many others already are.

But fitting in is boring,
You can't fit in when
You were born to stand out.
Every single person
An individual soul.
That can't conform to society's,
Unachievable norm
Because the norm can't exist
When everyone's different.
Embracing differences is
The unspoken birdsong to
Success, happiness, wealth?
To a life, I think.
To express yourself is to have a life
And with that everything else will come,

An attempt to fit in made in vain
Is time wasted.
An opposition of creativity,
And self-expression.

Identity doesn't define you as a person.
But you aren't defined by someone else's identity
Freedom in its many forms is the key to everything,
If you are willing to embrace individuality
And substitute repressed thoughts for self-expression,
To create a whole and original
You.

Matilda Wiggins (15)

The Storm's Reign

The cold has spread.
It blossoms on a defeated lung, grasping on the last breath, despite it knowing it's destined failure.
The water's menacing grip is relentless, violently tearing away the hope of life whilst thrashing without compassion, an innocent victim.
The rocks cradle, almost trying to save the despairing, but know they cannot interfere with the water's bloodlust, it's forbidden in its boundaries.
A salty tear cannot be seen in the inescapable depths of harsh, rapid blue...
Not even the rain dare threaten the swarm of water, but watches down in agony, as the final push of air escapes.
But as dim light softly falls from aghast pupils, your arm reaches into the aching abyss.
Your incandescent bravery shivering under the piercing glacial sting.
Once again, you raise from venomous depths,
Once again, you sing a lullaby to awaken the dismayed flesh,
Once again, you save me.

Jemma Crane

Your Tears In December

Your tears in January sing
the start of new beginnings.
They freeze on your cheek
as your joy is turned solid,
by her frosty touch

Your tears in February are hopeful
for a new tomorrow.
Reminiscent of the days past,
they yearn for more,
never knowing what.

Your tears in March fall with reluctance.
A numbness wells up inside of you.
Your heart is trapped
in a box of memories,
which slowly turns
into a coffin of shame.

Your tears in April shower the ground
with such a soft rain
You feel so guilty,
for this rain, so plentiful.

Your tears in May
drizzle onto the earth once more,
sharing their sorrow
with the soil.
How many days have passed like this?

Your tears in June
suffocate you.
You walk headfirst into raging traffic
without a care.
You cannot see,
you cannot breathe.

Your tears in July burn.
They tear your skin,
and collapse the dam of your resistance.
The flood eats you alive.
You can't take it.

Your tears in August roar
and tell a story of war.
An internal everlasting struggle,
seeming so eternal.
Left love scars
which covered your body and soul.

Your tears in September
remind you
of the tears of yesterday.
They console a crier
and they admire your beauty,
which never left.

Your tears in October
cast away the mist
which had sat in your eyes
for so long,
and guide you into the light,
from the darkness
which you had lingered in
for so long.

Your tears in November
tell you to relax,
and fortify your heart.
They mend a broken spirit
and reassure an angel
that its halo is made of gold,
not thorns.

Your tears in December are joyful,
and tell a tale of persistence.
They remember the tears of summer
and feel no regrets.

These December tears
tell a new story.
An end of suffering
and a new beginning,
full of self-love and hope.

Tomisin Olawepo (17)

To The Class Of 2021

Feeling passionate, enlivened, at the top of the world, is a feeling - ethereal.
To the class of 2021,
warmest wishes are induced, enhance your creativity, and broaden your horizons,
we've come so far, we've faced a year of the unfaced.
A liberty from this coconut shell, books and work crammed inside your homes -
but we've fought through it all.
To the class of 2021,
no matter which road you set foot upon,
no matter the distance
Let your heart guide your way,
the path is a long-intertwined puzzle but clear for a brave deer scarpering from its predator
chasing through nothing but achieving everything.
As it longs what it desires...
To the class of 2021,
be the deer, if you want to fulfil your dreams
Life was somehow delayed,
Remember the past cannot be changed but the future can be made,
the world is still out there.
Don't let the dark stop you,
don't let the flashing lights, the stop signs,
or the detours block your way of achieving what your heart desires.

Carry your knowledge forward,
light the lamps and don't be afraid to set the world ablaze
With the very steps you take,
cherish all the wonderful memories made
To the class of 2021,
remember you have a purpose, and it starts with you.
The starting line.
Who are you know, is who you will become.
Follow your heart and passions,
your goals
and conquer the impossible as you follow this path of life.
Congratulations!

Riva Sachdev (14)

Hope

Once I remember,
A place that I called home
A place with nothing but joy
A place with friendship and love

I could remember, the smiles on our faces
And the grins that infectiously spread through to our nostrils
And the myth that filled our hearts
With the songs that tuned our minds.

We were happy and we were warm
We were safe and we were sound
Everything was perfect
Everything was calm
Until it happened
Without a warning

Everyone was now in lust
Everyone was now in sorrow
We were trapped
And we were all alone

Our friends and families
Were long gone off
And our beautiful home
Was found no more

Our world was fell part
Like burnt charcoal

And still, no one tried to help

They turned their backs on us
Like stiffened monkeys
And continued to destroy us
With no hint of concern

I was furious but also worried
But I knew I had no choice but to have faith.

I just hope for a better place
A place where we can all be one
One in friends
And one in passion

I hope for a time
A time where we can all be happy
And a time where we can peaceful
A time where we can all be together
And a time where we can all laugh again.

Debbie Fadairo (11)

Stay Strong, Be Fearless

If you get bullied,
Just ignore what they say.
If you do a good deed,
Be ecstatic like the sun after a rainy day.

If you feel scared and apprehensive,
Make your heart stronger.
Stand up, try your best,
Go forward, and further.

If you feel that you can fly up in the sky to earn your dreams,
Remember nothing is impossible.
If you are given a task,
Take and finish it, make yourself responsible.

If you feel that you're having a 'bad day',
Tell someone about your trouble.
If you feel too stuck on something,
Remember, there is a light at the end of the tunnel.

If you feel that you're too 'exhausted',
Remember to keep on going and don't quit!
If you ever feel that you are up for the job,
Have a plan and go for it!

If you feel you're too small or as if no one gives any care,
Don't believe that, you can be one of the greatest people on the Earth!
Be as confident as a bird committing itself to the air,
Go and overcome the challenges that you'll find in your path.

Never think you are selfish, or powerless,
Give up anxiety, fear and feel your best.
Run, enjoy and feel fearless,
Like a strong tiger on its way to becoming the ruler of the forest.

Debaroti Choudhury (12)

Why Should I?

Why should I hide in the shadow
Because of the tan colour of my skin?
My tan colour skin is not what I chose,
It will be there and has always been.

No matter whether you are English, American,
African or Indian, we need to, now, stand up as one.

Why should I cower when they rise
To get up and challenge my birth nation?
The place that I was born in and where lies
My mother soil that gave me my foundation.

No matter whether you are English, American,
African or Indian, we need to, now, stand up as one.

Why should I only listen to the others
Just because I am an immigrant?
I should be allowed to speak amongst others.
Perhaps, we can have an imminent change?

No matter whether you are English, American
African or Indian, we need to, now, stand up as one.

It should never have to be anyone - me or you,
Who is forced to end up in such a situation.
To overcome this obstacle, we need to
Stop society from racism-creation.

We need to empower this change.
We.

Nalini Kailas Bhandarkar

I Dance, I Sing, I Cry...

I dance like nobody's watching
I sing like no one's listening
I cry when nobody's looking
This is me!

I give hugs when no one expects it
I smile when someone needs uplifting
I say I love you when it's most needed
This is me!

I jump up and down when I'm excited
I sleep when I'm exhausted
I run for miles when I'm frustrated
This is me!

I have mood swings when I'm unhappy
I share my love when I'm not snappy
I'd climb a mountain to help a charity
This is me!

I draw when I feel creative
I cook when I'm feeling bored
I cycle when I want to get fit
This is me!

I sit on the sofa when I'm feeling lazy
I walk my dog when I've got the strength
I water the flowers when my mum tells me
This is me!

Maira Soomro (9)

Who Am I?

I am cruel,
Who am I?

I am dreadful,
Who am I?

I send raging, grey, sharp fear through the sky,
Have you guessed?
Who am I?

If you listen you will hear,
Who am I?

Deafening bangs that burst your ear,
Have you guessed?
Who am I?

I smell smoke,
Who am I?

I am loud,
Who am I?

Through the years I've stood strong and proud,
Have you guessed?
Who am I?

I turn love into tears,
Who am I?

I have separated men for around four years,
Have you guessed?
Who am I?

All I am is fight, fight, fight,
Who am I?

And I give people a giant fright in the night on first sight with bright lights,
Have you guessed?
Who am I?

I am so bitter and sour,
Who am I?

Strangling people with fear every hour,
Have you guessed?
Who am I?

I am so happy this poem is over,
Who am I?

Know more torture as you read and saw,
Who am I?

For I am the one and only First World War!
Did you guess?

Andrey Nikiforov (12)

She's The One

It's the constant smile on her face even when things are tough
It's the above and beyond for every one of her students
It's the 100% effort she puts into everything to make things work

She is the one

It's the arriving at school in the morning ready to face a challenge
It's how much she cares and how much she wants to help
It's always being there when things don't work out for you

She is the one

It's the late nights after school to help people out
It's the time she spends making sure everyone is safe
It's the amount of second chances she gives instead of giving up on you

She is the one

No matter how many fights or arguments
No matter how many times I've called her names or been rude, she is always willing to make up and restart
She is and will always be

The One.

Miller Simpson (14)

Who Are We To You?

Who are we to you?
Are we people of colour?
The 'other' rich in melanin pigment
With big lips and kinky hair

The ones you only see in October
The ones you are forced to learn about one month a year
You love our food, music and rich culture
But us as individuals are irrelevant

Only useful when we score goals, carrying your team
But as soon as we miss, "Go back to your country!"
You compare our hair to an alpaca, tell us it's out of our unprofessional hands
But straight greasy hair is professional, right?

You mock us for what we were naturally born with
But then go on to replicate our features
We are humans too, not aliens.

Vanessa Uforo Nsikak James (14)

I Come From...

I come from crowded theatres to closed ones
Smiling faces to unchanging masks
I come from toxic friendships and unfinished words
I come from broken promises and unnecessary lies
I come from rooms filled with adults then empty ones
I come from lockdowns and Covid-19
I come from tears while looking in mirrors
I come from black and white pictures and wrong or right questions
I come from boredom and regret
But I also come from perseverance and dance lessons
I come from happiness and love
I come from hard times but coming out okay
I come from protecting the things I love
I come from doing my best
I come from believing in good over evil.

Kitty Knight-Spence (11)

Climate Change Catastrophe

Climate change is falling upon us like a blanket of darkness
However, hope is here to help us see through the darkness
Icebergs are melting
Water levels are rising
Australia's trees are burning
Co2 levels are increasing like wildfire
Australia's moving north 'cause icebergs are melting
Species of animals are on the brink of extinction
Catastrophic hurricanes of climate change effects swipe across the globe
Stop burning fossil fuels we all try to shout but our voices aren't heard.
Animal homes are lost due to modernisation
Greenhouse gas emissions increase like Covid-19 cases

Let's raise our voices, people.

Meenakshi Sri Hasini Jagarlapudi (11)

We Are Women, We Are One

To my fellow women around the world,
We are one, and one only.

No matter our race or religion,
No matter our size or height,
No matter who you are,
We are one and one only,
To sisterhood unite.

We are strong, we are powerful.
We fight and we sacrifice.
From suffragettes' heritage
To sisterhood unit.

From grandmothers to mothers,
From mothers to daughters,
With family ties
That bond for life.

We smile with strength,
We show scars of beauty,
We are amazing beings of achievement and skill,
Because of us the word is evolving still
We are all these things, and a whole lot more!

Darcie Wright (18)

My Voice

Oh, come on we can do this
Together we can make Covid go away.
We've been in lockdown quite a while,
It's really hard to make a smile
Future me, I wish there is no disease anymore
I just can't see people suffering.
I can't imagine the students of class 2021
Which wasn't at all fun!
I want to thank the doctors, nurses and scientists who are trying their best
Working all day without hardly getting any rest.
To let them work and figure out a task
We just have to social distance and wear our masks.
Just a week ago school started again
Finally, I'll not be annoyed or in pain.
Now I can play with my friends and reunite
We'll be safe and careful so we will not be in a fright.

Neelesh Gupta (12)

The One Left Behind

"I always love talking to you!"
You'd say,
Your voice echoing down the streets.
Your smile never failing to be there.
While we walked and walked.
Your eyes glistening in the sun
Your beauty was mesmerising.
I stared at you in awe as you'd say,
"I promise you won't leave,"
But promises are there to make you feel better.
I begin to finally realise,
As I walk down those streets once more.
The silence deafening within your laughter.
The road empty with your footprints.
My heart broken,
Without you there to keep intact.
And I am once again,
The one left behind.

Rabia Abdullah (14)

Empowerment

To control your life it can be hard!
Concentrate on what you want to do!
Your dreams can go higher than the Shard!
If you are diligent they can come true!

Life is a vessel ready to sail!
You steer the ship where it should go!
Sometimes things might fail!
You have to be resilient and then come back to flow!

In life you keep choosing!
So you have to be decisive!
It can be confusing!
That is why you must be incisive!

I want to be a scientist!
I want to be a superhero!
I want to be an archaeologist!
I want to be like De Niro!

This poem is about empowerment!
It's trying to reach your inner voice!
In life there is no dent!
Live it to the fullest and rejoice!

Darsh Kapoor (12)

Stage Fright

I need to get rid of all this fear
I only perform when no one is near
I hate doing things alone
When I perform, I feel like a statue made out of stone

I need to get rid of all this fear
I only perform when no one is near
Confidence is something I have never really had
But it is something on my list I would really like to add

I need to get rid of all this fear
I only perform when no one is near
I want to do things without fearing them first
I get butterflies and that feeling is the worst

I am trying to overcome my fear
To perform and not care if people are near
I won't be frightened, I won't be scared
That is final and let that be shared.

Zoe Mudd (11)

Cloaked Silhouette

She strode silently -
Like a swaying cloth of fine black silk.
Yet, whispers, sneers, and stares shadowed each step of hers.
The same unfading stereotypes persisted:
Suppressed, subjugated and brainwashed.
Or -
Ugly, timid and shy.
But -
Hear the words loud and clear:
She is a beautiful cloaked silhouette.
Freedom is sewn in a texture of her cover.
Ferocity sweeps in the depths of her vivacious eyes.
Beauty flows in the rivers of the heart.
Boldness clings to the soles of her feet.
She is a beautiful cloaked silhouette.
A 'phenomenal women' is who she is.

Hamna Ali (16)

The Sky

The clouds whooshing through the wind,
The birds pushing their wings to their limits,
When the bright blue colour of the sky goes away
The orange sunset colour comes in,
Then everyone goes home or some may be sleeping.
The bright sun has fully set,
The colour turns to the darkest night
But the moon stands out, reflecting the sun,
Making it the brightest thing in the night.
You see the stars like small white dots,
You see fireworks from a far distance, firing like rockets,
They shoot beautiful colours of beams of light,
Popping like hundreds of people clapping.

Milan John (8)

The Moon's Flower

There is something so impeccably beautiful in seeing a single flower brightly bloom.
Doing it alone, using a body as a home.
It makes me want to scream,
I am the only person who has always been there for me.
There is no need for fields of poppies or towers of staring sunflowers.
Your roots are deep below.
Trust yourself, for the lonesome can bloom.
Take it from the moon,
Draw breath alone, and you will also eventually grow.

Inayah Talal (14)

Doodle

Sometimes the words don't come out,
So I doodle.
Sometimes my pen can't stand words,
So I doodle.
Sometimes the deadline's today,
Nothing comes out of my brain,
So I doodle.
When my words wander astray,
I turn over the page
And I doodle.

It helps me build a character.
It helps me build a setting.
It helped me write this poem.
So when I'm stuck,
I doodle.

Connie Butler (11)

Future

Being careless
But not heartless,
Travelling to different places,
To sketch, paint or use the materials that are in my cases.

To help people with how certain things look,
Quickly sketching in my book,
Trying to get famous in a not normal way,
Luckily I won't have to work every day.

Being creative and free
But some might disagree,
Doing what I love,
Being like a free dove.

Lilli Stretton

Shackles

I saw the ecstatic physical phenomenon of my generation destroyed,
How I mourned the electricity.
Does the electricity make you shiver?
does it?

Why would you think the capacity is little?
The capacity is the largest ability of all.
A capacity is humongous. a capacity is macroscopical,
a capacity is enormous, however.

An electric, however hard it tries,
Will always be zany.
Electric - the true source of buzz.

Freddie Goodson

Imagine The World Was More Peaceful

Imagine the world as a better place.
We'd be free from problems like war.
We'd be free from any diseases.
There wouldn't be any violence and hurt
Towards anyone or anything.
The world would look beautiful
As nature would not get destroyed by people.
Everyone and everyone would be in harmony.

Kira Patel (12)

Power

Realities tie hand in hand,
like pink beaches with orange sand.
Words form across the page,
like a storm full of rage.
My mind wanders,
to thoughts that make me ponder.
A story told in many ways,
with a plethora of ideas it conveys.
There is no right or long,
everyone just goes along.

Sarah Curticean (15)

Imagine If The World Was At Peace

Imagine if the world was at peace...
No need for police.
No more bullies.
More opportunities.
No more heartbreaks in your life.
People wouldn't be walking around with a knife.
No more deaths in the world.

Pryan Kahane

Imagine England Won The Euros

Imagine England won the Euros...
We would go crazy.
Imagine we got knocked out,
We would all be heartbroken.
Imagine Kane scored a last-minute goal,
We would love him.
Imagine, imagine, imagine.

Lewis Holt (13)

Empowerment

Power, power, power
The absence of power is wonderful
Most people think the absence of power is a downer
But the absence of power makes you most powerful
But overall it leaves me feeling empowered.

Tyler Gumbo (12)

Empowerment

Empowerment is strength
Stronger than any muscles
If you have power of mind
You will win all of your tussles
Words are tougher than any knife
Knowledge is superior to taking another life.

Lewis Nelson (12)

Tormentor Of My Dreams

He arose from his king-sized bed,
With notions of ferocity in the head,
A wave of hostility and he sees red,
Without hesitation I turn to flee,
But not before he murdered me.

Amaan Shah (13)

Responsibility

The cat sat on the mat,
I hadn't expected that.
All these years without a pet:
It seemed my parents' minds were set.
But we took a call - what to do?
Here's a kitten in need of rescue.
A little kitten left all alone,
Waiting for someone to take him home.
Otherwise, he'd be left to die,
This was the moment to give it a try.
I'm now empowered with this responsibility,
This little kitten's happiness is all down to me.
He is so cute and very lovable,
He is also sweet and huggable.
He is so funny when he wants to play,
Other than that he will sleep all day.
Although sometimes he likes to scratch,
But it's his toy mouse he likes to catch.
He is always jumping on the tables.
We don't like it when he chews the cables,
After his food is out and he is fed,
He will sleep by my pillow on my bed!
When he goes to sleep what are his dreams?
Is it random or do they stick to a theme?

Does he dream about food and what to eat?
Or maybe his favourite delicious meat treat.
Does he dream about hunting and catching a mouse?
Or maybe just being let out of the house.
Does he dream about playing and jumping around?
Or maybe he just wants to keep his paws on the ground.
Does he dream about chasing a ball?
Or maybe cats just don't dream at all.

Zara Jenkinson (14)
Abbey Gate College, Saighton

Empowered

What is it to feel empowered?
Is it the feeling of strength?
Is it the feeling of power?
Is it the feeling of authority?
Or is it the feeling of being heard?
When do you feel empowered?
Is it when you are scaling mountains without ropes?
Is it when you are giving speeches to millions?
Is it when you are finishing first in everything you do?
Or is it getting an A in something you struggle at?
Who do you feel empowered with?
Is it at a round table with others who are brave and courageous?
Is it surrounded by the elite and the most talented?
Is it around people who you make laws for?
Or is it with people you enjoy the company of?
Why do you feel empowered?
Is it because you are the best?
Is it because you are in control?
Is it because you have the money?
Or is it because you have got a power?
No matter how big or small.

Billy Reynolds (14)
Abbey Gate College, Saighton

Stop

Stop running, stop running
Stop running away from who you are
Stop changing yourself for everybody else
Stop lying to yourself, just be you
Stop, don't be afraid to be who you are
Stop comparing yourself to everybody else
Stop wishing that you were somebody else
Stop telling yourself that you're not enough, you're beautiful inside and out
Stop believing what the haters say
Stop doubting yourself, you'll make it through this storm
Stop hating on yourself so much, you're perfect just the way you are
Stop worrying so much, just have a little faith
Stop beating yourself up about the little things that you wish you were
Stop telling yourself that you'll never amount to anything, you're incredible
Everybody else can see it, why can't you?
Stop wearing this coat of armour
Reveal the true you.

Maria Magalhaes McKown (13)
Abbey Gate College, Saighton

Empowered

In life, it's easy to just look back
And think about the things we lack
But little do we really know
The best things in life barely show

In life, it's easy to just compare
And look at things we may not share
But every time we look at others
We hide ourselves further under the covers

In life, it's easy to remember the past
And let old memories drag us last
To try and follow the paths of others
And forget to show our natural colours

In life, it's easy to hide our tears
And just give in to all our fears
It's clear to see we're all unique
So don't make normal what you seek

In life, it's easy to be afraid
And throw yourself into the shade
But next time you enter an interview
Just simply smile and remember to be you.

Oliver Hayes
Abbey Gate College, Saighton

Empowered

What makes you feel empowered?
For some people, someone is in their world,
Someone who they cannot live without.
It doesn't matter about colour or gender,
When love is out and about.
But not me.

For some people, they suffer a loss,
Of a person, a pet, and object,
And replacing that thing with something new,
They can sometimes feel complex.
But not me.

For some people, they were born in the wrong body,
They feel trapped, alone and upset,
And when they feel ready to change,
They get a different pronoun or sex.
But not me.

What makes me feel empowered?
People who are black, gay or Muslim,
Making the world full of diversity,
Standing up for who they are
And making their identity.
That makes me feel empowered!

Amy Reynolds (12)
Abbey Gate College, Saighton

Better Things

When I am sad I think of better things
I'm empowered by them
It helps me get through those things
People think that we must be the same, yet if everyone was
We wouldn't be unique
Unique to ourselves and different from everyone else
And then we stand out
Not for being a fake person but for being us
We must not be afraid of being who we choose to be
And not someone who the world forces upon us to be
When people don't think I can do something, I feel more empowered to do it
More of a desire to prove those people wrong and succeed
I want to prove them wrong for myself and that I am the opposite of what they may think
I am empowered to do these things
And that is why being empowered is better for every one of us.

Marcus Ettinger
Abbey Gate College, Saighton

To You

To people discovering this world,
You will face the unexpected,
You will have to fight for what's right,
And you will perfect what needs to be perfected.
You will make friends,
With different backgrounds to you,
From different walks of life than you.
You may have hard years,
But remember to power on, and stay strong
And push through your deepest fears.
When you're feeling down, things will always look up.
Keep positive and help others with the same attitude.
I don't know who you are,
But I do know that this advice will do you good.
Enjoy life and the world you live in.

Holly Gallagher-Lund (14)
Abbey Gate College, Saighton

Truth

She was not about to glue on the mask.
Or dance when she felt like screaming.
Carrying her confidence, she wandered away.
Not caring who caught up,
Or who followed.
She was not about to trade her truth
For any sense of belonging
She was her own woman.
Could take care of herself,
Emptied her thoughts along the way.
She was not about to sing for the man.
Puppeteers had tried to string her up already.
She laughed at their brazenness.
Not a care in the world,
Because she was her own woman.
Could take care of herself.

Daisy Lawson
Abbey Gate College, Saighton

Empowered

Relax kid,
You've got nothing to fear,
Remember your training,
Remember how you got here,
Relax mate,
I've known you for years,
The fastest kid I know,
You just grind through the gears,
Relax my friend, please,
I watched them warm-up
It may be the final,
And they're getting puffed up,
But it's clear to any bystander to see,
That they would easily lose,
Even to me.
Relax kid,
Just go do your thing,
And in just over ten seconds,
They'll see who's the king.

Xander Veal (13)
Abbey Gate College, Saighton

As He Stood There

As he stood there, seemingly alone, he didn't think he could.
Then he remembered,
The hours of training,
The skills gained,
The technique fine-tuned,
The practice followed by more practice,
Over the roar of his blood in his veins,
His coach's words of encouragement ringing in his ears,
His confidence soared.
Empowered by all that had gone before he realised he could,
So he did.

Jack Leatherbarrow (13)
Abbey Gate College, Saighton

Empowered

I look at the world
I see I am in chains
And I will break free
Break free to become successful
Without being hurtful
I will become empowered to be
The best version of me.

Luca Ralph (14)
Abbey Gate College, Saighton

The World Has A Plan

A sport where not one player takes a shot,
A game where everyone plays a part,
A tapestry when not one thread stands out of place.
That's the world's plan.
And society follows along, oblivious to the notion that we've labelled ourselves in the process - given ourselves parts we must play, in order to keep from being thrown to the outskirts.
And not one person understands that one day, someone will rise up to that plan, and break the long-lasting image we've labelled ourselves with.
Break the superior rule that binds us, that everyone has a part, and everyone should play that part accordingly.
I say not today.
Not today will I blend into the crowd, be the fragile, delicate girl the world thinks I am.
I'm ready to stand up, to show the world that these labels, these stereotypes we have blindly handed ourselves, limit our potential, as a nation, as a community.
And will consequently lead to the destruction of our stability.
The naivety of these people who have been corrupt with perceptions,
Will never rise to accept the people who put themselves out there,
The people who are different.
We are those people. You and me.

We stand out from the crowd because the world isn't made
for all of us to fit in.
This is my dream.
A dream of equality.
Of humanity.
Of love.
This is my dream.
What's yours?

Zara Thiara-Mahmood
Bourne Academy, Bourne

The Power To Choose

Like a goldfish
You swim aimlessly around
Not knowing what to do
And looking at others for what to do.

Like the clouds covering the sun
People cloud your choices
What's wrong? What's right?
The choices you make
But others don't want
Sometimes are different
And rarely the same.

Though the pros and cons sway your mind
Like a graceful blow
Or a beaming laugh
I would advise you to do what's right.
Just listen to your heart
Clear your mind
Don't look at judgemental eyes.

It's only for a little while, you may be happy with others' choices
But eventually, it will fall, frail and frightened.
Taking you somewhere worse than the highest of heights.
Though the right choice will hold strong and true
It will take you where you rightfully belong to.

Up in the clouds with the sun shining.
The birds sing and the future is so very bright.

Lucy Beaton (14)
Bourne Academy, Bourne

Dear Future Me

Dear future me
I have to tell you one thing
The life you live in could improve
The life you live in could worsen
The life you live in could stay the same.

Dear future me,
One thing I need to tell you
I am always with you
We are always together
I will never leave you.

Dear future me
One thing I ask of you is
Reach out to family and friends
Give them a ring
Visit them every so often.

Dear future me
I ask of you one thing
Believe in yourself
Be ready for anything
Be ready for nothing

Dear future me
One last thing I have to tell you
Never put yourself in peril.

Jadwiga Witczak
Bourne Academy, Bourne

I Shine

There is more than this.
I am more than this.
I stand tall against the horizon
Yet still merely a silhouette of who
I want to be; I am supposed to be.
Do you see?

I'm blooming with the flowers,
So wait for spring to come,
I'm not a shadow of me.
I am what's casting it, I'm like the sun,
I am burning with ambition.
So wait for me to rise,
Darkness is temporary, wait for me to shine.

Just wait for me to show you
All that I can be.
I am myself, and I feel it again.

I am me.

Elana Cox (14)
Bourne Academy, Bourne

This Is Me

Some say I'm silly and not important,
I say I'm fun.
Some say I'm lonely and unhappy,
I say I'm awesome.
Some say I'm messy and untidy,
I say I'm curious.
Some say I'm angry and annoying,
I say I'm passionate.
Some say I'm loud and rude,
I say I'm fearless.
Some will always be negative,
I say always be positive.

Jake Hellawell (11)
Bourne Academy, Bourne

Power And Hope

When I look at the world I don't see much hope.
Darkness fills me and it never stops.
When I see people showering their generosity,
it puts a smile on my face and the gloom I'm stuck in
gradually goes away.
The power people hold is not much to them,
but to my eyes,
it's something that helps.
I love when people don't take hope for granted,
it makes me feel like the world has a bandage.
I feel empowered when someone leads me
away from the darkness,
it gives me hope
and I tell myself, "I can do this."
I like it when the world is flooded with generosity,
it gives me power
to end this tragedy.
My smile
grows and grows from the power
this world holds.
This power will never go away,
I just need to pray for my
hope to stay.

Sedra Fawaz (12)
Hoe Valley School, Woking

The Final Few

Infinite problems consume us, binding us to our mortal sins,
We cheat, we lie, we insult and hurt, our darkness does begin.
Each person is poisoned with hatred, no matter how well they do not show it,
For each of us has been scarred from birth, and little to none knows it.
We are the judges of the souls around us, the masters to the feeble lambs,
In life, we hurt all that is good and pierce grief through our lands.
Destruction faces all that's just, despite its selfish rewards,
Light is shunned to our wicked eyes, as the things we love are scorched.

Only a handful of souls are different, and these are the angels of Earth,
They do not wish to hurt or harm, but hinder what it is we deserve.
In times of war, they protect us; in fear, they are our friends.
It is them who will heal us, and the world we have torn,
For we have infected this prosperous world, from the moment we were born.

From all the wrongfulness in the world, these people have remained,
Not tempted by evil, but for goodness, they are their slaves.

If it not for them we would have withered many years ago,
So long as they shall stand, we shall always have hope.

Shall you sit in famine; will you continue to laugh at despair?
Or shall you be empowered to join the last good people standing there?
Wait for a forgotten salvation, or be a part of the few,
Wallow in misery, ignore the wars,
Or fight for me and you.

Emma Smith-Gold (12)
Hoe Valley School, Woking

Us

I've been lonely for a lifetime but that doesn't count this day,
I could stay like this forever, 'til the stars come out to play,
I love you to the moon and back and to the ocean floor,
And just to see you laugh or hear you knocking at my door,
What happened to our younger selves? Are we so insecure?
I'd give every single thing I have to go back to how it was before,
The memories are all flooding back they put me in a daze,
But looking at the pictures, it's all turned into a haze,
I am me and you're still you, but only worlds apart,
And now that you don't love me, there's an empty space inside my heart,
My life's a mess, my tears still flow, my feelings caving in,
And still, the one thing on my mind is how you might have been,
This book, this room, this house, this place, reminds me that you're gone,
And that old jukebox in the corner, it still replays your song,
But now that you have left me, this whole planet seems so dull,
And every word that people speak, it turns into a lull,
The colour's drained out of my life and I just want you to see,
The only thing that held me to this earth was you and me,

You told me I would move on but I don't think that's true,
'Cause everything I ever did just brought me back to you.

Louise Heron (15)
Hoe Valley School, Woking

If I Had A Magic Wand

If I had a magic wand... I'd make HVS famous!
If I had a magic wand... I'd end this silly virus!
If I had a magic wand... I'd give the homeless a house!
If I had a magic wand... I'd feed the poor!
If I had a magic wand... I'd stop all crimes!
If I had a magic wand... I'd make the world a better place!
If I had a magic wand... I'd make my family rich!
If I had a magic wand...I'd stop racism! (We're all the same!)
If I had a magic wand... I'd end climate change!
If I had a magic wand... I'd stop all animal hunts and murders!
If I had a magic wand... I'd stop the pollution!
If I had a magic wand... I'd help the animals! (Just don't!)
And if I had a magic wand... I'd probably have to make more for my siblings too! (They're gonna want one too!)

Hadi Adalat
Hoe Valley School, Woking

Depression

I have a dog called depression.
He follows me around,
It led to much aggression.
I lost interest in the things I loved.
All of my family, I shoved
Right out the door, I was so ashamed
I couldn't be strong.

I went to a councillor to help with my worries,
My anger and all the quarrels.
Soon, I was better, better than before,
With the black dog on a leash.
I realise it happens to everyone,
But never again will I let it happen to me.
I could finally be strong.

Seek help, speak to people,
Or even a pet,
I want to help everyone with their black dog.
I know you are upset
All the time,
So was I,
But believe me when I say,
You will be strong.

Emily Nicholas (12)
Hoe Valley School, Woking

Empowered

Empowered what does that mean to you?
Well empowered
means to me,
power.
Like you can do anything you want
in this wide world,
like you don't have to be
afraid to speak up.

Say what's on your mind,
you don't have to feel sad or mad,
we want you to feel glad,
we want you to feel glad you're in this community,
we want everyone to have the same opportunities
to speak out loud,
let people listen to how you feel.
That's what empowered means to me.

Grace Long (12)
Hoe Valley School, Woking

Game Night

All snuggled up on the couch nice and warm,
We start with Monopoly which was a total bore.
Then we order pizza, a pepperoni feast.

Why don't we play Uno?
See who will be the best?
My dad won the game.

My mum won the fun.
While I emptied the bin, I said I was done,
Then my brother said he would win,
We played again and I won.
We packed up the games and finished the pizza,
We got ready for bed while my dad was shouting, "Beat ya!"
I got into bed and fell asleep quickly,
As game night was officially over for me.

Matilda Mills (12)
Hoe Valley School, Woking

A Smile That Doesn't Fit

Some people get their mother's hair,
Brown and flowing.
Some people get their father's grin,
Witty and glowing.

I got my mother's eyes,
Cold and blue.
My father's heart,
That said, "I never loved you."

Some people were lucky,
And got love and attention.
And I was left,
Feeling constant apprehension.

Some people say
That life is a gift,
But upon my face
There's a smile that doesn't fit.

I needn't be reminded,
I deserve it, I do,
But what's it like
To be told I love you?

Darcy Kane (14)
Hoe Valley School, Woking

Being A Woman

Being a woman isn't as easy as it seems,
Having the constant feeling that someone is after you,
But why? Why women? What have we done?
Why is this so sad but true?

Why do women who work certain jobs still get paid less than men?
Why is this still an issue?
Why be so unfair because of gender?
Women are still people too.

In fairy tales, why can't the woman protect herself?
Why does she need a man to save her?
Why is it seen as 'unladylike' to fight?
Why is it seen as wrong and not right?

Inaya Dar (12)
Hoe Valley School, Woking

You Don't Own Me

You cannot tell me what I can or cannot do,
You can't tell me what to wear.
I am my own person, I'll choose
What is best for me.
You don't know what I feel comfortable in or what I feel confident in.
I will marry who I want, Father.
I know what is best for me, Mother.
I will talk to whoever I like, husband or wife.
I will say this once more,
I am my own person!
I decide what is best for me.
Why?
Because I am not a prize to be won!

Cleo Lewis (14)
Hoe Valley School, Woking

Being Me

Being me is something I can't describe,
Being me is very different,
Seeing life through my eyes,
Not being a person who is very confident.

Being me is very strange,
Being me is okay,
Always wanting to change,
But realising that how I am is okay.

Being me is sometimes confusing,
Being me is sometimes fun,
Doing things that can be amusing,
Doing things like going for a run.

Being me is just being me,
And being me is being free.

Abigail Sakyi (11)
Hoe Valley School, Woking

Lantern Wishes

Haiku poetry

Slowly the sun sets,
Everything has gone silent,
Cherry blossoms fall.

A girl all alone,
Sitting in her kimono,
Watching the stars fly.

Lanterns float above,
Shimmering up in the sky,
Filled with hope and life.

Bella Aziz Manious
Hoe Valley School, Woking

Starstruck

I've always wanted to be like the stars.

It sounds ridiculous, I know,
but the idea of having someone stare for hours;
admire your beauty,
ponder your meaning
and seek safety in your presence,
is oddly comforting to me.

But lately, I've noticed the stars don't shine quite the same anymore -
they've lost their shine,
they've lost their spark,
and yet they're still burning bright,
unbeknownst to the naked eye.
A mighty ball of gas hard at work,
unnoticed,
overlooked,
and yet still doing its job.
A flame burning to a degree that only few will ever truly understand.
Perhaps I am closer to the stars than I originally thought.

Hope Beirne (16)
King Edward VI High School, Stafford

Mother

Dear Mother,

Thank you for telling me to pick myself up no matter the pain,
To continue no matter what because in the end, it'll all be okay
Thank you for giving me the strength to ignore the shame
You showed me how to smile even though I lost the game

Thank you for a shoulder to cry on
For showing me how to have to the elegance of a swan
Thank you for showing me how a hug can protect me from every doom
Thank you for showing me how to be in full bloom

Thank you for showing me how to accept myself for who I am
Now I show myself as colourful and loud
And now I stand proud
Now I will announce myself in a crowd

Mother, you made me proud

Thank you for making me so proud of who I am
Thank you for showing me how to empower
Thank you for not letting me be overpowered.
Thank you for showing me my superpowers.

Munsimar Kaur (12)
King Henry School, Erith

Destiny

Destiny is a pathway
Beyond imagination
With no retreats nor regrets
You were made with a goal
A goal to fulfil in life
It does not cost a fortune
But costs your belief and courage.

Success Alonge (12)
King Henry School, Erith

Empowered

When I am angry, I feel empowered
Even though it turns terribly soured.

When I am angry, I feel no pain
Funny thing is, being angry has no gain.

All through the strain, the plain and the vivid vision of what I've become
I see and think, what a terrible son.

It's almost like an eerie stun
It's like being shot with a dull gun.

Everything you thought was fun is now tossed in the moment
You need to be calm before all you love is lost.

Patrick Filmer (14)
Lakeside School, Chandler's Ford

Ebony

There's no denying
the army is rising
the black race is fighting
thunder and lightning
some feel the only way to fit in is lightening
the way they make their hair
"Ha, look what he's wearing, over there."
Represent your country in what you wear
he's wearing handmade West-African material
why do we feel the need to be serial
killers of our own people's ways?
Why can't we just accept how people portray
themselves? Be yourself, no one else
maybe she's not the richest in wealth
but her heart is pure
and her skin is empowering
are we all equally powerful? Yes, I am 100% sure
so we all raise our fists and stand for each other
because she's your sister and I'm your brother.
There's no denying
the army is rising
the black race is fighting
thunder and lightning.

Alhusien Barrie (14)
Our Lady & St Chad Catholic Academy, Wolverhampton

Mother, Oh Mother, It's Winter

There's snow outside
don't want to go
but Mom insists
hands gone numb
feet are wet
scarf fluffy
hat scratchy
I wish I could go back
back to my nice warm bed
electric blanket
keeps me warm
blanket forts keep me happy
brother keeps me company
Mother makes me calm
nice warm supper
keeps my stomach warm
the warm feeling of family
it's buried deep down
my mother and siblings
staring into an abyss of technology
but when we are outside
the joy of family
playful family

when there is snow outside
snowball fights, snowmen
and snow angels
it fills me with glee
oh Mother, can't there be snow all year round?
Or just a couple of months
a couple of weeks?
Even a couple of days
just the playful family
the family is all I want
just play and play
all day
or not, I'll fall
fall into an abyss of loneliness
loneliness that I can't escape
oh, Mother, you save me from everything
Mother, oh Mother, you are my superhero
your love is stronger than all the superheroes in the world
I love you, Mother
you too, Brother
the winter is as painful as a splinter without you
Mother, oh Mother, I love you to the moon and back
your love for me is beyond the love that anyone gives
anyone.

Joshua Brookes (11)
Our Lady & St Chad Catholic Academy, Wolverhampton

The Key To Our Success Is Confidence And Hard Work

Let go of the thoughts that don't make you strong,
Because you should know you're enough.
You will be who you work hard to be,
Someone that has a right and is free,
Someone that takes that difficult but not impossible step,
Who everyone must respect.
You'll become the light,
That'll inspire others to fight,
You'll become the hope,
That'll inspire others to grow.

But if you give up,
You'll fall behind,
You won't be on the top,
And will be undermined.
I admit there are always some twists and turns,
But that's how everyone discerns
The meaning of fearlessness,
After embracing their worthiness.

Be like the itsy bitsy spider,
He's just a tiny animal and never gives up,
While we're humans,
And still can't keep up?

At the end of the day,
Hard work always pays off,
In every possible way,
As confidence is the key.

Remember, be confident and be stronger,
Until you can and maybe for even longer.

Jaspinder Atwal (13)
Our Lady & St Chad Catholic Academy, Wolverhampton

The Match

As the game began, the crowd started to cheer,
it was the first game in the whole year,
this was the big game,
I had to have my best aim,
as I saw the players step onto the pitch,
I knew we couldn't be left in the ditch,
the adrenaline started to run through me,
the referee started to count one, two, three,
the ball was kicked, the game had begun,
it was one to none,
I knew we were going to win, until
I got a strange chill,
the team began to score goal after goal,
once more the ball was stolen,
down to the last half - we had to score,
we had to get one more,
we started to play at our best,
this was my quest,
the goal was scored, it was over it was done!
A smile shot up on my face,
I was happy that we had won,
I looked the players in the eye
and wished them a good day,
the players looked pretty grey,

I assumed they were tired,
and walked off the pitch.

Raymond Wilcox (11)
Our Lady & St Chad Catholic Academy, Wolverhampton

My Parents Are The Universe

You gave me life, you let me dive into a world of paradise
You're both a living beauty and have a hard duty
You read to me tales about castles and kings
Read to me stories of many more wonderful things.

You fed me and fed me more and more
Until I got stronger, stronger and stronger
Now look at me, a fabulous little boy
Writing a poem about my fabulous Mum and Dad.

I have fallen off my bike many times
When I look up I see your cute giggle
You help me up and take care of me
Cuts and cuts, plasters and plasters.

My love for you is as big as the universe
And I can tell yours for me is even bigger
You say you will love me until the day I die
And I will always say right back at you.

This is why my parents are the universe!

Prem Harbias (11)
Our Lady & St Chad Catholic Academy, Wolverhampton

Halloween Night

It is a dark night,
Halloween is in my sight.
Young children running with candy,
costumes looking alright,
I see Frankenstein, zombies, and way much more,
it couldn't be a better sight.
Bright orange trees swaying left and right,
oh, someone's rung the doorbell on my overdecorated door.
I wonder what it is, trick or treat?
Bright lights everywhere, I'm going down the stairs.
I've opened the door but no one's there!
I close the door and I stare!
I walk away as it is bare!
Going back to my room,
It's eleven o'clock, I am watching Halloween movies in doom!
I fall asleep in my bed and when I wake
I notice it's almost December
so Christmas is next...

Maddox Henry (11)
Our Lady & St Chad Catholic Academy, Wolverhampton

Witch's Brew

The witch's spell,
made the others smell

the witch's broom
made the principal swoon

the witch's cat
couldn't have sat,
especially when there's a rat

what's to do in a world full of -
I'm not gonna finish that, heh

her shoe turned into a rock
as the others started to mock

her hair turned green
it was definitely to be seen

her arms were long and broken
the words the others wanted to say were unspoken

her lips grew small
she became very tall

"What's wrong with her?" the principal said
well, it was the witch's spell.

Hannah Chytra (11)
Our Lady & St Chad Catholic Academy, Wolverhampton

That One Dream

You know, if you have
a dream, go for it
does it matter what people think?
Nope!

When I was seven, I actually
wanted to be an actor,
but back then I was scared,
I didn't like when people looked at me!

What's your dream? Really?
Wow! I love that job,
you know, I also wanted
to be a drama teacher.

When you're young, you change
your mind a lot when it
comes to a job,
like I did probably wanted to be
about one, two, three, five, eight, nine...
Oh no! I mean,
a lot of jobs.

So it proves, you can be
anything!

Scarlet Yates (13)
Our Lady & St Chad Catholic Academy, Wolverhampton

The Great Skateboard

Feeling the breeze rush through my hair,
Hitting the ramps and getting air.

Grinding the rails and riding around,
Listen to my wheels. Oh, what a wonderful sound,

Doing heelflips, kickflips and pop shuvits too.
I could never find anything else to do.

While going on a ramp so high,
I thought that maybe I could fly.

I fell off my board with glee,
As you will truly see.

It didn't hurt you or me
Because it was a trick you see

And now it's time to say goodbye,
While I am going super sky high.

Logan Blakemore (11)
Our Lady & St Chad Catholic Academy, Wolverhampton

School

I wake up in the morning,
And get myself together,
I instantly get a warning,
That there's not gonna be the best weather.

I put on my uniform,
And tie my shoelaces,
I can hear the thunderstorm,
As I pack my pencil case.

I walk into my classroom,
With my headphones in,
Wishing I was in my bedroom,
As I wait for my lesson to begin.

Voices come from left to right,
As I sit there with a frown,
People say school is fun, positive and bright,
But if only they knew what really goes down.

Ruth Mushangwe (12)
Our Lady & St Chad Catholic Academy, Wolverhampton

My Future Self

Dear future self,
One thing I hope for
Is to inspire girls to play sports.
One thing I dream for
Is to raise money for charity.

Dear future self,
One thing I hope for
Is to make a difference in women's sports.
One thing I dream for
Is to not be embarrassed about being bad at things.

Dear future self,
One thing I hope for
Is to be good at sports.
One thing I dream for
Is to prove that girls are good at sports.

Maddison Fellows (13)
Our Lady & St Chad Catholic Academy, Wolverhampton

Why Is It Important To Be Yourself?

Some days, you forget what it is like to be gentle
and look at yourself with kindness.
Others will trick you into believing you are not
good enough, but you are, you always
have been and always will be.

You are beautiful, magical, successful, strong and confident.
You were born to be real not to be perfect, 'cause
loving yourself is the key to happiness.

Be your own reason to smile 'cause life is too
short to be someone else.

Isabel Uzochukwu (13)
Our Lady & St Chad Catholic Academy, Wolverhampton

The Star Is In The Night

The star is in the night
shining bright
way up high.

The star is bold
there are stories to be told
down below.

The star is in the night
shining bright
way up high.

The star is loud
nice and proud
in the crowd.

The star is in the night
shining bright
way up high.

The star is about to burst
be prepared for the worst
don't you worry, because there's more that lurks.

Gracie Pickin (11)
Our Lady & St Chad Catholic Academy, Wolverhampton

Everyone Is A Love Poem

Everyone is a love poem.
A walking one.
Not for everyone, but only the ones that adore them.
I look out of my window and see people,
many of them, walking, running and talking.
They are someone's love poem, today or tomorrow.
They know, but they might also not know.
Isn't that a beautiful thing to realise?
How gentle it would be if we treated those love poems with care and trust.
Maybe then this world would be a book with a good ending.

Emilia Samek (13)
Our Lady & St Chad Catholic Academy, Wolverhampton

Human Fights

Everyone join the fight,
The fight to give everyone the right,
To help raise and not sink,
The right to think,
The right to love,
The right to do everything and more above,
No matter if you're gay or an ally,
If you're truthful or love to lie,
Black or white,
Fight day and night,
Abled or disabled,
Deaf or blind,
I hope that one day we will all be of the mind,
See everyone is equal,
We are all mankind.

Caitlin Foyle (13)
Our Lady & St Chad Catholic Academy, Wolverhampton

To Me, Remember Me

Remember me, this is to me,
It was that day, they say,
She had a smile that stopped the sunray,
He had tears of joy,
It was a baby boy,
To me, remember me,
On that day of March,
We were born,
Remember the little things that brightened her days,
Remember the talks that made him proud,
And I say this out loud,
I love you, Mother and Father,
You made me go further,
I hope for you,
To me, remember me.

Koshan Harbias (13)
Our Lady & St Chad Catholic Academy, Wolverhampton

The Fans Are Back!

The fans are back in the stadium!
The atmosphere is electric,
jeers and cheers from every fan.
Faces filled with sheer delight.
Eyes of the children light up with joy,
adults chant with intent to motivate their team.
Moans and groans in frustration hit the players every time
they misplace a single pass or shot.
Passion visible wherever you look.
Oh, I am sure glad Covid-19 is on rampage no more,
the fans are back!

Shebuel Nyagota (12)
Our Lady & St Chad Catholic Academy, Wolverhampton

Made Our Banner

They say Black Lives Matter,
but our blood on their hands makes me sadder.
They kneel and post,
and then they like,
all the cases are suddenly closed.
We overpowered the oppressors once before,
so we are going to say BLM until there's no more
killing, attacking, unnecessary searching.
We made our banner
when we said enough is enough.
One will say we finally won.

Natalie Ndongala (13)
Our Lady & St Chad Catholic Academy, Wolverhampton

The Chocolate Poem

Chocolate is falling out of the machine
Happiness is created
On the moon, astronauts can smell this delicious scent
Created and filled with joy, makes people cry with happy tears
Of course, everyone loves chocolate
Loved by the creators as well
All day and all night people will sneak chocolate away from others
Teachers can't resist chocolate
Everyone adores chocolate.

Callum Picken (12)
Our Lady & St Chad Catholic Academy, Wolverhampton

Kobe Bryant

Kobe Bryant is an inspiration
He was kind and generous
He was nice and caring
He helped shape a generation
He was the best basketball player before he passed away
He changed people's lives
He played for the Los Angeles Lakers
He died, sadly, in a helicopter crash
It upset a lot of lives
Basketball was his dream
Which he was the one to achieve.

Jayden Jackson (11)
Our Lady & St Chad Catholic Academy, Wolverhampton

Green

Stop the world burning,
Bring it back to green,
Keep the air happy,
Keep the air clean.
We can stop this,
So we can have green.
Keep the world healthy,
Have our lungs clean.
Since global warming,
Is ruining our trees.
So plant more with me,
To keep us alive.
Since my life matters,
And so does yours.

Tegan Connoly-Birch (11)
Our Lady & St Chad Catholic Academy, Wolverhampton

The Day Of Halloween!

H appiness begins with Halloween
A llow the kids to come running
L aughter and
L ove all around
O nly on Halloween
W hen the nights go dark
E ntries become breakable
E ven for the ghosts but
N ot on Halloween.

Freya Oldfield (11)
Our Lady & St Chad Catholic Academy, Wolverhampton

Winter Day

As you sleep in your bed,
Snow falls from the sky gracefully.
Poor cats freeze in the white, fluffy snow,
As dogs run around chasing tiny bugs in homes.
Bunnies sleep in their homes,
As bears fall into a deep slumber.

Sharon Szombath (11)
Our Lady & St Chad Catholic Academy, Wolverhampton

Take A Breath

Here we are, sitting with pride,
But out there another black soul has died,
Breonna Taylor, George Floyd and poor Tamir Rice,
All for being black, they had to pay a price.

From slavery, we have come,
Yet there's still injustice,
Deaths from racial abuse,
We need to rise above it.

From Minstrel shows
The blues was born,
Rapings and assumptions,
Loving families torn.

Who gets the blame
For any ounce of crime?
Who are the ones suffering
And sitting someone else's time?

But, how many times
Can we make the same mistake?
We think ourselves so clever
But all we do is destroy and take.

So what are we going to do?
Sit and wait,
How many more lives are at stake?

Ebony-Grace Williams-Goodman (14)
Parklands Academy, Chorley

Happiness

Happiness
There are certain things that make a person happy
For some, it is a person
For some, it is a game
Some, a movie.
For me it's rain
People say rain resembles sadness
Loneliness
For me it resembles stillness
It's like the whole world stops
When I'm standing in the rain getting drenched to the bone
It's like all my worries wash away
And instead of my clothes absorbing the water
My body is absorbing happiness
Joyous and free
So rain is happy
Still
Never sad and lonely
Because the dancing raindrops will be there
Dancing and singing
Splishing and sploshing
Alongside side you.

Anabel Sorbie (13)
Parklands Academy, Chorley

Haiku About Stupid Moths

Dark and cold outside,
And so warm and bright inside,
Therefore, I go in.

Oisín Whitehead-St Pierre (12)
Parklands Academy, Chorley

Dear Past Self, I Will Always Remember

To my past self,
Times are hard but never will I give up
You'll find the one who won't break your heart.

Sometimes I take a breath and go into another land,
Where all my problems wander around.
I take my time but don't always complete what I plan to do.
I always make sure that my family is safe.

Dear past self,
I breathe but don't talk.
I see but I don't believe.
I think but it is never true.

I always overthink.

Dream on, dream big
But don't always dream the impossible.
Times are better but not always good.
You can think what you want but not what you need.

Your dreams don't always come true.

Your dream to be a poet, you have accomplished.
But you didn't save your brother.

He becomes more rude to you,
You raised him but he'll always look up to you as his saviour.

Dream big little one as you'll always the bright side of the bad.
Never let go as they'll hold your hand,
You'll always see what brings greatness to your life.
So don't give up.
Never be let down.
You'll be one or the other but never both.
Stay strong I'm in your heart.

George Brade (14)
Plumstead Manor School, London

Welcome To Society

Welcome to society, a system we made.
A place where freedom is, only in certain ways.

You can live however you want to,
But it needs to be to our taste.

You can say whatever you want,
But too much and you'll be shut away.

This system is full of caring people,
Who only care for themselves.
But they do look after you if you pay them very well.

A brilliant ideology to live in unity,
But only the powerful have more equality.

Is it not wonderful to live in such a world?
Where corruption and poverty is free,
Where saving a life or teaching to live one costs a fee?

Welcome to society, a system we made
And there's only one last thing, you can't escape.

Falak Afroz (12)
Plumstead Manor School, London

Wolves

We sit alone prepared to feast
No thought to who partakes,
Ignoring battles fought within
Creating more heartaches

And yet 'alone', we never are.
Inside us battles roar.
Two wolves competing for our will
Each enemy's at war
Both strong and fierce with awesome might
Yet more diverse are they.
One wolf will whisper how you've failed
To make your critics pay.

He stirs the anger kept within,
Adds greed and envy to the pot.
Self-pity and some arrogance,
Resentments not to be forgot.
The other wolf is joy and faith,
Compassion, love and peace,
Benevolence and empathy,
Goodwill that will not cease.

Both hungry beasts await your will.
Decide which wolf you need.
For you alone dictates who dies
The one you chose... you feed.

Asevini Arunthavanatan (14)
Plumstead Manor School, London

Making It In Life

You must do anything possible to make it in the future,
You may go through a lot of torture either good or bad,
If you know you want to be successful in the future,
You must do good things and the right things to reach there,
You might have an obstacle on the way but do not let that stop you,
If you go to the tabernacle to pray to God to help you,
He would help you if only you help yourself.
You might be prey but strive to be a predator,
Do not be in fear but be prepared,
If you are not the only one that wants to reach there,
Just know you have won.
It might be unclear to you but always know you are near
And you will later reach there.

Elizabeth Kukoyi (16)
Plumstead Manor School, London

Proud To Be Me

24th of January 2008 I was born
When I woke up it was dawn
I got up
Got dressed
Then I thought to myself, *I am blessed*
School is hard
I am trying
But inside I am dying
For my family I'll do everything and anything
Being good for Mum and Dad
Wanna make them proud not mad
Dreaming of football
The crowd cheering
But there is always one thing I am fearing
Hate
It's always about the colour of your skin
Or whether you're thick or thin
Whether you're black or white
One day we will all get the respect that's right
Discrimination is wrong
BLM we all stay strong.

Charlie East (13)
Plumstead Manor School, London

I'm Tired

I'm tired
And that's okay
But it's eating me alive
The pictures haunt me every day
I'm tired
And I want a break from the reality
But if I escape I'll find all I think about is fatality
I'm tired
And all I want is rest
But no matter how much sleep I get
There's always something on my chest
I'm tired
In my mind or in my head
I don't know which words to use
But the feeling haunts me in my bed
I'm tired
Of having to keep things to myself
But letting it all go feels like placing the insecurities on a shelf.

Lacie Arnold (15)
Plumstead Manor School, London

No Strings Attached

I picked up the paper,
Still trying to escape her,
For now, all that I know,
Is that I have to hide,
Hide, hide, hide.
I hated when she lied,
Just to impress her friends,
She made me feel all tied.

We used to be best friends,
At all odds and ends,
But now all that we were,
Is nothing but strangers,
Strangers surrounded by dangers.

But, hey,
That is okay,
Because even at bay,
When you enter the doorway,
New people to meet,
For there will always be,
Someone good enough for me
For me and you to be.

Delia Padurescu (13)
Plumstead Manor School, London

To My Future Self: Be Ready

Dear past self,

Open your eyes and see the truth as friends will soon come through.
You may not see right now but in time you will.
Don't close your eyes till you see that the truth will reveal what you want.

I'm from the future and times are good.
So don't let yourself down.
Think of me when you're young and old,
You can change the future not the past.

Lay in bed till you see
A whole new world is waiting to be discovered by you.
So be ready for a bunch of adventures.

I am the future don't sleep.

Olamide Demehin (13)
Plumstead Manor School, London

My Future Self

Dear future self,
How have you been?
Happy or sad?
Well I might never know
Only in the future I guess
Do you like what you are doing for your job?
Are you a doctor or a nurse or maybe a fashion designer?
Are you married to a nice guy?
So many questions fill my head,
I don't know what to ask.
Well I guess this is goodbye for now,
I will write soon again,
Bye-bye.

Sowmini Arunthavanathan (12)
Plumstead Manor School, London

Your True Identity

Life will get better
The sooner you see the better it will be
Don't let anyone control your life, be free
All you need to do is believe
Then you'll achieve all your dreams.
You're the only one that knows what you want
Be confident in yourself
Life will get better.

Anam Aziz (16)
Plumstead Manor School, London

Dear Future Me

Dear future me,
I want you to promise me just a few things,
when times get hard I want you to pick yourself up and dust yourself off.

Dear future me,
Whenever your dreams feel impossible, unreachable, a mountain climb away,
promise me now that you will keep on trying and never give up.

Dear future me,
Always have confidence, even if it's a challenge sometimes,
speak out, not just for yourself but for the people who cannot.

Dear future me,
If you feel like you're tied up to a chair, you can't speak and you've lost all hope of being free, persevere, persevere until you achieve what you need, what you want, what you feel.

Dear future me,
One thing I ask of you, just smile, don't hide behind a mask,
don't act like you've disappeared, just smile.

Dear future me,
Remember it's you, it's you who has the strength you need,
it's you who has the power to make a difference.

Sadie Farrow (13)
Salford City Academy, Eccles

Dear Future Self

Dear future self,
I ask one thing of you,
Spend time with your family,
Tell them you love them, they need it.

Dear future self,
One thing I ask of you,
Recognise that life gets better when it gets hard,
Remember to always pick yourself up,
Speak up for the weak and for those that don't have a voice.

Dear future me,
I ask one thing of you,
It's okay to be different,
Be who you want to be.

Dear future me,
One thing I ask of you,
Remember to share things that make you happy,
And happy, you will be.

Imogen Farrow (13)
Salford City Academy, Eccles

Dear Future Amber

Dear future me,
I ask of you
To be true to yourself.

Dear future me,
When life gives you lemons
You make lemonade.

Dear future me,
Even though life might be hard
You try your best and gleam.

Dear future me,
Don't put the mask on
Be who you are to me.

Dear future me,
Reach out to family, ring
Pick up the phone and bling.

Dear future me,
The last thing I ask of you
Prepare for life
There are going to be obstacles
Live life and sing.

Empower to be yourself!

Amber Silcock (13)
Salford City Academy, Eccles

Dear Future Me

Dear future me,
One thing I ask of you,
Follow your dreams, no matter how bad things seem,
Remember to try and see them through.

Dear future me,
I ask of you one thing,
Never give up, however tough it feels,
Pick up the phone and give your family a ring.

Dear future me,
Another thing I ask of you,
Always have a smile on your face,
Don't let anyone ruin your happy place.

Dear future me,
The last thing I ask of you,
Always have a smile,
I promise it will be worth your while.

Maisie Hughes (12)
Salford City Academy, Eccles

Music Producer

M aking your head free
U sing instruments to your heart's desire
S inging out your inner heart
I nteracting a dream
C hasing your inner goal

P rocessing life choices
R elying on people to save you
O pening your heart out to the world
D reaming about the future when in the past
U sing family and friends by your side
C asting opportunities above you
E valuating the past now it is the future
R evealing all secrets.

Blake Woodley (12)
Salford City Academy, Eccles

Dear Past Me

Dear past me,
Check on your nana, she loves you so much,
Love all your family even though there's a bunch.

Dear past self,
Love your brothers, give them more time
It does not cost a penny or a dime.

Dear past me,
Your parents adore you
All you need to do is open the door,
Do not be sad with your mum and dad.

Dear past me,
That is all there is to say,
Live your life, it will all be okay.

Joshua Houldsworth (12)
Salford City Academy, Eccles

Empowered Family

Father, Mother, Brother, Sister,
Warm, cosy house, watching TV
Games, eating snacks and crisps
Getting new furniture,
Making cheese on toast,
Much love.

My mum, dad, brother,
Making me hot chocolate and marshmallows.
Never give up on family.

My family is my world,
Mother, Father, Brother and Sister.
We all love movie nights on Fridays.
We love family time.

Charlie Hanlon (13)
Salford City Academy, Eccles

Father, Mother, Sister And Brother

My family provide heating
They keep me warm
They cook me food to keep me warm
My brother keeps me warm with a blanket
My sister keeps me warm

We go on trips
We enjoy life together as a family

We have takeaways to eat
We have Christmas dinners and they are great
As we eat the Christmas dinner
We open the Christmas crackers.

Ryan Smith (12)
Salford City Academy, Eccles

Empower

E is for empowerment
M is for making a difference
P is for having power over yourself
O is for originality
W is for working hard
E is for encouragement
R is for remembering who is boss.

Elizabeth Cunningham (12)
Salford City Academy, Eccles

Dear Future Me

Dear future me,
One thing I ask of you is,
Always be happy,
Even if you're not.

Dear future me,
One thing I ask of you is,
Always be high,
Even when you're low.

Kara Taylor (12)
Salford City Academy, Eccles

Matthew

M ajestic rugby player
A lovely personality
T ragic at football
T remendous at cooking
H elpful person
E xcellent student
W orks hard.

Matthew Ryan-Jones (13)
Salford City Academy, Eccles

Free Bird

I like to fire an arrow
I wish I could fly like a sparrow
I want to be free
I want a house in a tree
I like to eat worms
I live in a world full of germs
Please help me!

Matthew Houareau (13)
Salford City Academy, Eccles

What Is Empowerment?

Perhaps empowerment is to wear your heart on your sleeves,
and instead of pecking beaks of daws,
tender hands hold your muscle that believes,
holds your virtues, mind, and flaws.

It could be your thoughts that form into bubbles,
holding them in your palm and letting them pop on paper
with words that carve into your soul and troubles
that as you write, slowly taper.

Maybe it's streaks of paint on black canvas forming
figures, shapes, wisps of breath that play
out in the minds of souls that look upon it, warming
the soft crevices of their heart as they wander away.

Possibly, it's still walking - crawling, even - on morning fields
or concrete paths, not knowing when the horizon will end,
who you'll bloom to be, and what the future wields.
A star in the sky flowers, though, and you choose to wend.

You call this star Purpose, and it makes a home in the sky.
Some days it's brighter than the sun, some nights it's not even there.
Yet, it still watches in love even if there's nothing to descry.
It hopes you still keep on going, even when you're in despair.

Perhaps empowerment is still not giving up,
even when life doesn't seem enough.

Anastasija Stradniece (17)
Solihull Sixth Form College, Solihull

If I Could Fly

If I could fly, we would easily discern the world
Shimmering towers that beam.
If I could fly, we would have an aerial perspective
Of relics and stacks that gleam.

If I could fly, I would take you with me
Soaring above the stars,
Over dazzling oceans and mountains and seas
Depositing our turbulences afar.

If I could fly, we would be more ethereal than feathers
Scudding the grass and water with our hands
Because, indisputably, even being aloft
And not enchained cannot ameliorate
The perilous woes of our incensed land.

Emily Docherty (13)
St Paul's School For Girls, Birmingham

Our World Is Dying

Our world is dying
And it needs help reviving.
It is mandatory to reduce, reuse, recycle
To give it a higher chance of survival.
Natural disasters can occur anywhere,
But they cause damage everywhere.
People are the cause of these muddles
And the government are doing nothing to ease these troubles.
Mother Nature is beginning to retaliate,
We are the source to assassinate.
So we must nurture our home,
To let the animals roam.
Our world is going to suffer,
But we will assist and help it to recover.

Anjelica Rosaupan (12)
St Paul's School For Girls, Birmingham

The Gallery Of Art

Walking through the path of October
Many figures who have changed the lives
Hanging on the walls smiling as seen closer
As the golden frame glitters as it appears.

Appreciate them for their good deeds during their lifetime
Generation after generation they still are being admired
Within the caption: 'When people are determined they can overcome anything in time'
Their eyes gleamed with the compassion being inspired.

Walking through the hallway of monumental people
Another caption: 'You must never be fearful about what you are doing when it is right'
They followed the way of bringing change with treacle
Within the darkness they became the moon within the night.

After that journey we recap
Everyone is equal but different in their own way
Nelson Mandela, Rosa Park and many more
Became our map to guide and care for the youth every day.

As Martin Luther King Jr rightfully mentions: 'The time is always right to do what is right'.
These people have worked hard to gain the rights of humanity for everyone.

Ritthyha Kumanan
Sydney Russell School, Dagenham

Feelings

Look at me, a happy girl
But my life may look like a complex math question.
Sometimes my feelings sink down like water in a tap,
Sometimes my feelings look up like a balloon in the sky.
I am black and I do suffer from racism
But I ignore those ones and look on the bright side.
No one is perfect.
Not everyone is respected.
We can change this world.

LGBTQ+, let's support it,
Don't sit around and do nothing.
Racism is happening out there, let's not abuse it,
Let's help them.
Different religions?
Let's respect them.

Look at me a happy girl
But my life may look like a complex math question.
Sometimes my feelings sink down like water in a tap,
Sometimes my feelings look up like a balloon in the sky.
I am black and I do suffer from racism
But I ignore those ones and look on the bright side.
No one is perfect.
Not everyone is respected.
We can change this world.

We all do and look at things differently
But we do not judge them.
Take hobbies, for example singing,
Dancing, drawing and sports.
School and jobs might look hard
But if we look on the bright side
And keep things organised, we will make it!
Never give up!

Look at me a happy girl
But my life may look like a complex math question.
Sometimes my feelings sink down like water in a tap,
Sometimes my feelings look up like a balloon in the sky.
I am black and I do suffer from racism
But I ignore those ones and look on the bright side.
No one is perfect.
Not everyone is respected.
We can change this world.

See us now.
There is now peace.
Now let's be friends until the end.

Nancy Bampoe
Sydney Russell School, Dagenham

Black Is Not A Bad Word

Black is not a bad word so why is everyone avoiding it like it is?
Everybody around me only just started talking about inequality
Must fight twice as hard to get something right in front of me
Black is not a bad word and oppression is not just a mindset,
It's systematic racism designed to cause offence.

Black is not a bad word because we've all got the same pink flesh
It is who I am and what I am proud to be
A huge portion of my identity.

Black is not a bad word and Black Lives Matter is not an ideology
It is a movement to fuel progression
So that our children will not face the same oppression.

Black is not a bad word, and it is not a trait or a characteristic
Because every black person is different
It is not something to be whispered behind someone's back
Because being black does not equate to being bad.

Black is not a bad word or a preference
Because no one chooses to be a minority
Your voice swallowed by a white majority.

Black is not a bad word
It is a colour, a people
A movie with a sequel
Because we're moving forward to a scene where life is more equal.

Ruth Ogbuokiki
Sydney Russell School, Dagenham

A Girl With A Voice

I am a girl who is eleven,
At seven I used to think this world is just like heaven.
I get furious when you tell I'm not serious,
So please do not call me delirious
You say that you listen and hear
But you haven't noticed me for over a year.

I am a child and my voice might be mild
But I am free and wild
And I will continue to keep my smile even when I'm running a mile
Because I have power and a voice,
And no, it's not just background noise.

So take a seat and listen
As I share with you a part of my vision
As we avoid all future collisions.

PS I am not depressed
I just want to address
What I would like to protest.

Edona Krasniqi (11)
Sydney Russell School, Dagenham

Who Am I?

My name is Elisa Gjoka.
I love the colour purple.
I am a sister to two brothers.
I am also a daughter.

The team is called Army Cadets.
That's where I belong.
Dressed in camouflaging colours.
We are all always having fun.

I go to Sydney Russell School.
I am great at making friends.
I find myself cool.
But I'll never make friends first, as I like to observe.

You'll always find me reading
Or cooking with my mum.
But you'll never find me pleading
Or doing my own chores.

Think of me as nice.
But never mean or rude.
I love who I am
And where I belong.

I don't think I'll ever change!

Elisa Gjoka (13)
Sydney Russell School, Dagenham

You'll Be Fine

You'll be fine,
Sometimes you might feel sad
Or even mad,
But you should be glad
That you are here.

People can be mean
But you are a queen.

Sometimes you might get anxious
But you can still be righteous.

Sometimes you might become depressed,
Like a dark shadow is looming over you,
But others are still impressed by you every day,
Whether it's because of how you draw,
Write or express yourself.

No matter how you feel today
You will always come out of it okay.

You'll be fine.

Stacie Croitoru
Sydney Russell School, Dagenham

We Are Here Today

She has the power
To make a difference,
She has the creativity
To make a change.

She has the strength
To make her voice heard,
She is the reason
We are here today.

He has the willpower
To say, "This is wrong."
He has the skills
To speak aloud, like a song.

He has the hopes
To reason with others this present day.
He is the reason
We are here today.

Together we can make a difference,
Together we can change our world
For the better.
This is the reason,
We are here today!

Amira Ali (11)
Sydney Russell School, Dagenham

Win

They said I was a loser
They said I will never win
But I always lost
Just because of my skin
They always cursed me
Because of how I looked

And when they scared me
I was shook
They called me a wimp
Because I always cried
When I wanted help
No one was on my side
I tried to run away
Run away from my fears

But I couldn't
I had to handle my fears
All I had to do was confide
But I only lied
After I did
And was now done.

I'm not a loser
I was the person that won!

Ra'id Sadik
Sydney Russell School, Dagenham

I'm Human Too

Why are they shocked?
That I hate being interrupted
No one likes it
I'm human too.

Why are they shocked?
That they need permission from me for a picture
No one likes having their picture taken without permission
I'm human too.

Why are they shocked
That I feel sad and angry?
I have emotions
I'm human too.

Why are they shocked
That I love sweet treats?
Lots of people love it
I'm human too.

Rishmile Khan
Sydney Russell School, Dagenham

I Am Strong

I am not the smartest,
I am not the best,
I am not competitive
But I am still strong.

I am good at maths,
I am good at sports,
I am good with my hands
And I am still strong.

I am not the kindest,
I am not very helpful,
I am not nasty,
But I am still strong.

I am good at acting,
I am good at listening,
I am good at electronics,
And in total, I am still strong.

Kevin Gjoka (11)
Sydney Russell School, Dagenham

Friendship

People come and go,
Friendship grows,
Friends share their darkest secrets
And never tell a soul.

They make you laugh
And make you smile,
It's a special relationship
That grows and never stops giving,
And makes life worthwhile.

Haleema Bhatti
Sydney Russell School, Dagenham

What Is It About Our World?

What is it about our world that racism exists?
What is it about our world that terrorism exists?
What is it about our world that anti-semitism exists?
What is it about our world?

What is it about our world?
That us 'humans' are seen as monsters,
Our women being raped on our streets,
And our children seek shelter

What is it about our countries
That racial injustice exists?
Black people being wrongfully imprisoned
Due to the colour of their skin

What is it about some people?
Blinded by their advantage,
Many affected by anti-semitism,
And many stripped of privilege

Is this the world we truly live in?
Is this the world we really breathe in?
People dying up and down,
Yet we sit and make no sound

Instead of us coming together
Joining our hands as one
All we do is sit and watch
Whilst innocent lives are gone

Why don't we all empower ourselves?
Stand together as one,
What is it about our world
That makes my brain go numb?

Adebola Adeleke (13)
The Academy Of St Nicholas, Liverpool

Over And Over

Over and over the doubt seeps through,
The uneasiness envelops me.
Over and over the anxiety seeps through,
Uneasy about who I'm meant to be.

Should I be like them or should I be who I want to be?
Over and over the thoughts sweep through,
The crystals on the bedside release their aura,
Over and over the sadness sweeps through,
Uneasy about who I'm meant to be.

Should I tell them yes or should I tell them no?
Over and over the guilt peeps through.
Alone with my thoughts devouring me,
Over and over the frustration peeps through,
Uneasy about who I'm meant to be.

Taking a breath each sharper than the next.
Over and over anxiety hits me,
Each person saying 'calm down',
Over and over the resentment hits me,
Uneasy about who I'm meant to be.

You're a girl, not a gender,
Over and over the irritation pushes me
I can't be me because I have to meet their standards,

Over and over the stress pushes me,
Uneasy about who I'm meant to be.

Raven Scholes (11)
The Academy Of St Nicholas, Liverpool

Different

We're all different.
Different sizes,
Different shapes,
Different heights,
Different looks.

Society's beauty standards,
Doesn't bring joy,
Doesn't bring happiness,
Doesn't bring hope.

Being a model wouldn't make you happy,
They have insecurities too,
They will always look up to someone else
Thinking they are 'prettier' and more 'beautiful'.

Throw away the strict diets,
Obesity and stretch marks are beauty too,
No matter if you lose the weight and get to your 'beauty goal'
You will always think you have a flaw,
People will still try to bring you down.

So why not end it,
Make you you.
Live life to its fullest,
It doesn't last forever.

We're all different.
Different sizes,
Different shapes,
Different heights
Different looks.

Skye Ainsworth (11)
The Academy Of St Nicholas, Liverpool

Dear Future Me...

Dear future me,
Try to work your hardest
And achieve your goals.

Dear future me,
Try to reach out and keep in touch with others
Especially your friends and family.

Dear future me,
Try to achieve your dreams
And don't give up when things are hard.

Dear future me,
Try to be more confident about yourself
And try to be happier for yourself and others.

Dear future me,
Try to be more positive
And be more healthy.

Dear future me,
Try not to return to who you were in the past
And to not go back to people who hurt you so many times.

Dear future me,
Try to love yourself more
Before caring and loving someone else.

Remember to do something today
That your future self will thank you for.
All of your scars from your hard work and battles
Are what makes you unique and beautiful.

Alexis DeLuna (13)
The Academy Of St Nicholas, Liverpool

Be Happy Be Grateful

Be happy
Even if you're having a bad day,
Don't hold a grudge
Even if you're unhappy.

Be happy for your family
If they have success, it's a good thing,
Don't be jealous,
Good times will come.

Be happy for the good things
That bring you confidence.

Be happy when you come home
To your loved ones,
Many don't have that.

Be grateful for your own identity,
Every person is unique.

Be happy,
Think about the atmosphere around you
That brings a good mood and joy.

Be happy,
You have gratitude in your own self
That you can show.

Be happy
That you put a smile on everyone's face
When they feel sad.

Be proud of yourself,
For successful achievements you have achieved.

Be proud,
Try and put a smile on everyone's face.

Adriana Krajevskaja
The Academy Of St Nicholas, Liverpool

Frozen

Frozen in this eternity
Your saccharine cherry blossoms play in your mellow sanctuary
Your damp mist soaks into my stone shell

Your brittle buds emerge into adulthood, watered by your love
Your amber rays warmly kiss my cold mask
Yet still imprisoned in your emerald chains

Your golden feathers descend from the heavens
As I watch your lights rise and fall
Your haunted cries echo throughout your wooden pillars
That yearn for the clouds
Your once vivid artwork washed away by time

Your tone saddens as trees are stripped of their wonder
Daggers of ice formed from your shivering tears hang from my crystal body
Your green shackles shatter, freeing me from my torment
Only to be held by your cold embrace once again.

Catherine Daly (13)
The Academy Of St Nicholas, Liverpool

Where I Used To Be

I used to get bullied 24/7
Now I'm on my knees praying to Heaven
Wishing that it could stop
But deep down it's not
Telling my mum every day
I try explaining in every way
Her not believing me makes me sad
I used to have friends but then I had one
I don't have any now because that one is gone
I cry and cry and sob and sob
Wishing that it all could just stop
"You have to be like us!"
"You have to be tough!"
No I don't. You know I'm not tough!

21 years on...
I have been placed with a crown
I didn't need to be tough,
I didn't need to be rough,
I am normal, I am who I am.
If you don't like it, this is your time to leave.

Ruby Hargreaves (11)
The Academy Of St Nicholas, Liverpool

Empowered At Christmas

On Christmas Eve,
Eager to get my presents I'm about to receive
We put up the tree,
Red and green is all you can see.

Put the tinsel around the living room.
Then later on we gaze at the moon.
Waiting for Santa to eat his pies,
Because we have not told any lies.

As family are coming home,
Oh look I've just found a Santa gnome!
Soon after we decorate for Christmas Day
As being jolly is the way.

I enjoy a Christmas dinner,
The lights have just gone dimmer.
As I put the wreath upon the door,
Then I pick up a present off the floor.

As the snow begins to fall
I hear Santa call,
People now wear gloves, scarves and woolly hats
As they sit on the bench watching the cat.

Grace Allen (11)
The Academy Of St Nicholas, Liverpool

Dear Future Me

Dear future me,
Always be happy.
No matter what you go through,
Friends and family will be there for you.

Dear future me,
Become whatever you want to be.
Even when you feel like giving up,
Know that you are enough.

Dear future me,
Always be free.
Never feel sad,
Because things are going bad.

Dear future me,
Know you are worth it,
We have come so far from what we were.
Do everything to be happy, find your place.
And stay there for as long as your soul can take.

Dear future me,
Don't give up just yet.
If you fail get back up,
There are just setbacks, obstacles in your way.
Try and try again, don't ever stop fighting
Because you deserve it.

Cara Lamb (14)
The Academy Of St Nicholas, Liverpool

Ho Ho Ho

What would happen if Santa forgot
To come to your house on the dot?
No presents there for you to see
And you would be sad, not full of glee.

So to help Santa to come to your house,
Bed early for you, be as quiet as a mouse.
Leave out some food on Christmas Eve night
For Santa to eat and Rudolph to bite.

When you wake up early on Christmas Day
You'll see all the gifts he left on his way.
Santa is very special so treat him well
And he'll come back again, you will tell.

If you want him to remember you each year,
Then say out loud with a Christmas cheer,
"Santa, please leave some gifts for me
As I've been as good as a boy can be."

William Bowen (11)
The Academy Of St Nicholas, Liverpool

Summer Sun

A summer sun,
A ray of light,
Shining bright,
A bird taking flight.
There was a girl,
In a pink dress,
She twirled around,
Feeling like she was levitating away from the ground.

Looking up at the sky,
It seemed to be so high,
One day I will be up there,
Roaming in the air,
I will rule victorious.

The dress glistened in the sun,
The children ran enjoying the fun,
They twirled around in joy,
The sky was as bright as a lightbulb,
The tides of the sea were our rivals,
The sun shines in our faces like the flare of a candle.

The meadow was grassy
The breeze was mellow and happy,
The flowers bloomed,
The different colours created paradise.

Sophie Barnes (11)
The Academy Of St Nicholas, Liverpool

Environment

One day someone was walking through the woods,
He saw litter on the floor
He tried to pick it up but no, there was more!

Loads of broken glass,
Loads of toxic gas,
Loads of plastic bags,
Loads of broken ink pens.
When will this world go back to normal again?

Loads of animals are dead, I wonder why.
It's because we don't care, but why?
It's because we can't be bothered, right?

Please don't litter.
Please don't lie.
Help the animals
And save their lives.

So people please listen,
Before our future dies,
Please spread this word
Please, right now!

Scarlett Brown (11)
The Academy Of St Nicholas, Liverpool

Pick Yourself Up

Embark on an adventure
Leave early for a departure
Have fun, don't linger in the past
Leave the trap you have set yourself
So don't finish it yourself.

Pick yourself up
Don't think about that cup
Don't set up the rope
Go ahead and abandon that memory
Don't make another enemy.

Leave the chair by the desk
Don't go to the rooftop
Make sure you don't drop.

Leave the pills for when there's a need
Not yet, the time to feed
Go and see the sights
Go see the Northern Lights
So pick yourself up, and go get friends
So you don't end up by yourself.

Albert Manzu (13)
The Academy Of St Nicholas, Liverpool

The World

Outside is such a wonder
With buildings, dogs, cats and thunder
History throughout the years
Works very similar to cogs and gears
We live in a world with monsters and creatures
But the real freaks live right here
As animals evolve and change
The extinction leaves humans to blame.

As this planet keeps us spinning
In the evolutionary war, we're winning
With every tick-tock of the clock
Brings us closer to the fire, so hot
As we pollute the cold outside
Many creatures have curled up and died
To you, my brave listeners,
Could you give the world more care?

Owen Kelly (11)
The Academy Of St Nicholas, Liverpool

Magic

When you fly high,
High in the sky,
Make sure you don't fall
You won't like that at all.
But you won't do that,
Magic will make sure of it
But use your powers for good,
Is that understood?

Fight for humanity,
Stop great tragedies.
Magic will help you,
So fight fair and true.
But that is not all that magic can do.

Even in the worst of times,
We will stop these horrible crimes.
So use your powers for good,
Is that understood?

Fight for humanity,
Stop great tragedies.
Magic will help you
So fight fair and true.

Laura Connolly (11)
The Academy Of St Nicholas, Liverpool

Alone

A woman's worst fear is the dark,
The gut-wrenching feeling of being alone.
Walking in the dark alone is terrifying,
The feeling that any minute you could be whipped away.
The feeling that someone is lurking behind you,
How are we supposed to feel safe if policemen do it too?
Speaking out is mortifying,
It's the chance that no one will believe you
And you could ruin his life
But nobody gets that he ruined mine.
Women shouldn't feel alone, women should feel safe.
What has happened to the human race?

Evie Hunter (14)
The Academy Of St Nicholas, Liverpool

Manchester Trail

M ysterious
A nxious
N ot knowing why
C an't find where my heart is
H eart's spread apart
E nvy dancing in my mind
S o many choices to pick - how will I decide?
T rails and rails all around
E nvy buried deep underground
R ail or fail

T racks and facts
R un and hide or decide
A nger crawling everywhere
I don't know but I don't care
L ove is dug into my heart and my decision is finally made.

Jennifer Pearson
The Academy Of St Nicholas, Liverpool

Dear Future Me

Dear future me
Please don't give up on your dreams
Stay in touch with family
Don't give up on friends
Don't care what other people think of you

Dear future me
Be positive
Be passionate
Be healthy

Dear future me
Do things that make you happy
Do things that make you feel alive
Do things that make you feel confident

Dear future me
Try to stay positive
Try new foods
Try to work your hardest and achieve your goals

Dear future me
Don't give up on yourself.

Joel Smallwood (14)
The Academy Of St Nicholas, Liverpool

Hopes And Dreams

Hopes, hopes, that's what I need
To guide my way and see where it leads.
My hopes are big and my dreams are bright,
Let's hope this will go without a fright.
My dream is to become an amazing lawyer,
If I try hard enough I won't falter.
This is the job I want to succeed in,
That's the one I want to be in.
Hopefully, this will come true,
If I try hard enough, it will come through.
My dreams are gonna be real someday
Let's hope this will go without a day.

Janet Walker (12)
The Academy Of St Nicholas, Liverpool

High In The Sky

The blue sky
A beautiful sight to behold
Some have dreamed
Some have seen

It's different when you're in here
Confined to the small space
The cockpit
All the controls
At your hand
Some have dreamed
Some have seen

The electrics keep you alive
At 20,000 feet
When the blue sky turns grey
And fire engulfs some
The unfortunate ones

Bullets fly through the air
They whizz past
But that's not what matters
What matters is you're high in the sky.

Evan Campbell (13)
The Academy Of St Nicholas, Liverpool

Who Am I?

Who am I?
Who am I to change how I act?
To read, hear lies spat at my face about a concealed truth.
Who am I to not believe as I'm a witness.

Who am I?
Who am I to be cuffed in chains?
Stereotypes spread and drilled into the brain.

I am not an individual.
We are a process yanking on chains,
Lifting the boulder over the mountain.

We are the people,
Not animals locked in cages
Brains going through phases.

Jesse Smith (13)
The Academy Of St Nicholas, Liverpool

Bullying

When you're falling into an abyss
Remember this.

When you're running out of hope
I'll throw you a rope.

When bullies are bullying you
Remember you'll get through.

Life is a test
But you're the best!

When you're at a dead end
Just think of me, your friend.

Never say never
Because you are better.

And if that isn't enough,
And things are getting rough
Remember, you are tough!

Azher Naiju (11)
The Academy Of St Nicholas, Liverpool

Equal Rights

Think about all of the people who are not as wealthy
Think about the people who cannot afford.

Think about the people who do not have food,
Think about the people who do not have water.

These people deserve better,
These people deserve more.

If you think of you
And then think of them,
If you think of how you live
And think of how they live...

We can do better.

Thomas Green (14)
The Academy Of St Nicholas, Liverpool

Future Me

To future me,
What will I be?
Hopefully kicking a ball on a pitch
And being really, really rich.

The dream for me
Is to play for PSG.

Be their world-famous striker
Kitted up with Nike,
Much better than Mbappé
Who on the ball is rapid.

I can score 300 goals
And take on multiple roles.
I am empowered to be me,
Just you wait and see.

Kane Towers (11)
The Academy Of St Nicholas, Liverpool

Don't Look Down

Maybe I won't be scared
Worrying I'll be bullied
Hoping I'll have friends
Scared I'll get lost
Hoping I'm not the weird kid
What if I get left behind?
I want to be the popular one but won't
Now I'm going to be truthful to myself
Thinking positive to myself
Keeping my head high up
Being the best
Making friends.

Maizie Martin (11)
The Academy Of St Nicholas, Liverpool

Red

Red is a sunset
Blazing at night.
Red is being brave
With all your might.
Red is laughter,
Love and passion.
Red will never
Go out of fashion.
Red is warmth
You get inside.
Red is emotion,
A feeling of pride.
Red is standing
Ten feet tall.
Red is the greatest
Colour of all.

Keira Slack (11)
The Academy Of St Nicholas, Liverpool

My Old Self

I used to be small.
I used to be unable to talk.
I used to be unable to walk.
I used to crawl.
I used to roar!
But now I want to walk out the door to see my dog.
I used to pet my ted.
I used to sleep in a bed.
But now I sleep on a mattress.

Louie Edwards (11)
The Academy Of St Nicholas, Liverpool

My Name Is Magd

My name is Magd
And I like football
I don't get volleyball.

My name is Magd
I am what I am
I like what I am
I like what I do.

My name is Magd
I love my family
As long as they are with me.

Magd Naji
The Academy Of St Nicholas, Liverpool

Dear Future Me

Dear future me,

I have questions,
Can you help me?
Am I tall,
Taller than Mum?
Am I a gamer
Or is it just for fun?
I've just started high school,
What comes next?

Harley Allan
The Academy Of St Nicholas, Liverpool

Boxing

Boxing can be good
Boxing can be powerful
Boxing can be bloody
Boxing can be hard
Boxing can be painful
Boxing can be hard-working.

Freddie Kenton
The Academy Of St Nicholas, Liverpool

My Snow Boots

My mind concealed itself from the world for a moment,
distant and burying itself within its deepest untouched thoughts,
for I do not wear my snow boots often
but the cold descent of the Earth's winter coat called upon me to don mine.

My winter coat enables my ponderous habit
in its burdensome weight upon my shoulders,
and as I haul my snow boots beside the footpath I cannot help but covet the heat of the summer,
when I may prance and pirouette gaily in my summer dress.

Perhaps it is simply that thought that allows me to remove my winter gloves,
allows me to discount the burning of the frost at my fingertips,
allows me to carry a much lesser weight as I amble along in the thoroughfares of London.

But my feet remain confined within the laces of my snow boots,
a tireless reminder that the sun shan't protrude the white of the fog and cloud for yet another season.
The weight of my winter coat, only there to ridicule any hope I may have spared.

But I torment the furred creatures upon my toecaps and prepare myself for departure;
I must remain aware of the awaiting faces, nothing but a train journey away,
and I hope that they do not notice my winter coat, among their summer dresses.

My winter coat that depresses a mass around my swollen cheeks;
my swollen cheeks, no longer bitten red from the cold;
my swollen cheeks swelling with the warmth the shafts of sunlight amidst the blue provide;
I decide, upon reflection, my dependency laid down on my woollen scarf
is no longer of use to my swollen cheeks.

My snow boots singsong tirelessly against the sizzling pavement,
and as they detoured the length of the carpeted labyrinth,
I finally don my summer dress.

Tobias Riegler (13)
The Crypt School, Gloucester

The Different Things

When you feel down,
don't frown,
you are a good person.
If you're a bit different from everyone else,
it's fine,
you are a good person.
If you get bullied,
it doesn't matter,
you are a good person.
If someone is mean to you,
they are in the wrong
Because you are you,
you are special,
and that's who you are.
If you're in hospital from a horrific car crash,
and you're scared you might die,
remember all the happy moments in your life,
because you are a good person.
If you're suffering from abuse,
and you feel like you're being used,
remember, you can always ask for help,
even trying is excellent,
because you are a good person.
If you've done a piece of work
that is out of this world,

and your teacher gives you a reward,
feel delighted!
Feel ecstatic!
Be proud of yourself!
Don't let ignorant and brainless bullies
bring you down
and shred all your confidence up.
Because you are you,
you are special,
and that's who you are.
And no one can change that.

Zakariya Anwar (12)
The Highcrest Academy, High Wycombe

Bottling Up

When keeping secrets,
Life can be tough,
Trying to tell someone
You're feeling quite rough.

Could be depression,
Or a thought down below,
You're feeling so lonely,
Your happiness at zero.

People always say,
"Look on the bright side,"
But they don't appreciate
How you're feeling on the inside.

Mental health is important,
But they don't understand,
The world swallows you up,
And you can't stand your ground.

But just take this advice,
As the future is near,
Tell someone you love,
Before your hope disappears.

Elise Meredith (12)
The Peterborough School, Peterborough

Us

Who is society if not me?
We are all society and so are all guilty
Who are we to judge?
When we do nothing
Why do we try to be different?
For no one in particular
You're saying you're doing it for yourself
And you might well be
But who told you that you have to be that way?
That shape
That kind
That type
To be happy

We are all one big family
Community
We are all different races, abilities, societies, classes
But where will we be in the end?
All our bodies will be six feet under
Or in a precious jar on a mantelpiece
We might have made an imprint
A difference
A tiny dent
Or we might have left nothing
Maybe no one
Maybe someone will remember us

But who are we really, to be looking at ourselves
And thinking they're better or I'm lesser
Or I'm better and they're lesser?
We will end up in the same position
Heaven or hell
Whatever you decide
Whatever you believe
Will people remember us, or will we be forgotten in a minute
A month
A year
A century?

Why are we hung up on tomorrow or yesterday when all we should be living for is today?
We'll get to tomorrow soon and yesterday is gone
Forever
All we have is the present, a real gift in itself
Value it
Love it
Think of it as a prize
Own it
Your world
Their world
Our world to make, to shape, to create
Your world is completely unique
You see it only through your eyes
Nobody is seeing exactly the same thing as you

Feeling the same as you
Your world is yours to enjoy.

Araoluwa Aina (12)
The Peterborough School, Peterborough

Pieces

Why should it be this or that?
Why has one always got to be better?
Cancel the ones who don't suffice.
I tell you once, I tell you twice;
This isn't right, the way we fight.
Why not all as one? Why not all together?
Why must we all fight, until we reach the end of our tether?
What is this rush we create to divide?
Why can it only be kill, and if not, die?
Why not in peace? Why not together?
It shouldn't be so hard,
Just to put the pieces back together,
From when we broke our society apart.
All of us, so different,
And yet, we stare at the same moon, the same sun.
So, what on earth makes people murder, just for the cause of fun?
People cannot control their race, nor their sexuality.
So, let them be, it's none of our business, and that's plainly the reality.
Religion, income, politics, age;
Don't speculate, don't discriminate.
For the different beliefs may not be yours,
But nonetheless, each has a cause.
Let us not disturb the tranquillity of life,
By piercing through diversity with a knife.

For diversity is what makes us unique.
So, let us believe what we want to believe.
Just let us live in peace.
Who cares if we are different?
Who cares if we are not the same?
That is the point of life, so let us not shame.

Emily Emre (13)

The Peterborough School, Peterborough

A Poem About The Pandemic

In 2019 when the pandemic started,
Many people started to die without breath,
Some are alive but in hospital with Covid positive

In 2019 when the pandemic started,
A huge amount of people died with Covid,
Then they started to wear masks and use sanitiser all day.

In 2019 when the pandemic started,
People stayed at home which is called quarantine,
Some people didn't believe in Covid,
And just go out and then come back with Covid and die.

And now in 2021, children started to go to school as if they think Covid is gone,
The mask and sanitiser is used a little,
But some people still use masks and sanitiser to protect themselves,
From the dreadful virus called Covid-19.

Kevin Saju (11)
Watford Grammar School For Boys, Watford

Back When

Back when today seemed so far away,
Back when I lived happily without a problem in the world,
Back when my sister, Willow, was alive and well,
Yes, those were the days, when I was a newborn babe,

I lived happily with my mother and father in a cloud of bliss,
But this was just the calm before the storm,
A few months later, my mother and father went their separate ways,
But after that came a golden sky when a man named Ashley became my new stepfather
And my dad met a woman by the name of Abi, who became my stepmother,

But then I learned that lightning can strike twice,
I was five years old, and the story you are about to be told still brings a tear to my eye, though I try to be bold,
My sister, Willow, fell gravely ill, she was rushed to hospital, but never came back,
I will never forget the memory of her lying unconscious upon the floor that morning,

But, once again, a miracle would happen,
Two years later my mother gave birth to a daughter, followed by another two years later,
And in the year in-between, my stepmother gave birth to my eldest half-brother,
And two years later gave birth to another newborn babe,

So take it from me, no matter how dark the clouds, how fierce the rain, the sun will come out, to brighten your day,

You've just got to believe, just one tiny bit,
You just have to focus on the sun hiding behind it,
Because deep down, we all know something that is true,
That we all are able to do one special thing,
To know that we can do anything,
That you can climb the tallest mountain,
That you can overcome any challenge,
But most of all, that you are empowered.

Kian Casey (12)
Watford Grammar School For Boys, Watford

You Can't Blend In When You Were Meant To Stand Out

You do not let your guard down for life
You never cover your heart because people could despise
You do what is right and never tell a lie
You do it all because you could make someone smile

You could make days brighter than the sun could
And you could share life with people who love you
And when people try to judge you
You stand strong 'cause you were meant to

So life isn't a game
Let's just try to not make it lame
It was meant to be led in a good way
But some never want to change

So let us practise what is right
Every day and every night
God appreciates those who are kind
To be healthy you have to have a good mind

I'm sure we all make mistakes
And we all know it awaits
For every single one of course
We have a source

But there's something more to it that is clear
You can't blend in when you were meant to stand out.

Shaan Mohamed Shiyam (12)
Watford Grammar School For Boys, Watford

To My Family

To my family,
I just want to say,
Even through our darkest of times,
Your smiles always make my day.

To my family,
You all are my heroes,
When I'm feeling down,
I'll never be a zero.

To my family,
You treat me like a king,
You nurse all my tears,
You heal all the cuts - and the ones that really sting.

To my family,
When I'm with you,
I feel like I'm over the moon,
I know for a fact I love you, and I know that's true.

To my family,
Hear this one last thing,
For me, you sacrificed everything,
Your love is like Picasso making art,
And your compassion is like music made by Mozart,
When I'm trying to say is, Mum and Dad, you two will forever be in my heart.

Shaanthrigan Nisanthan (11)
Watford Grammar School For Boys, Watford

New Eleven-Year-Olds

To all the eleven-year-olds who started secondary school,
Let's face it,
Embrace it,
We are now the high schoolers,
The tough two years of lockdown,
Let them go,
Don't let them make you frown.
Just because today you feel different,
That predicament
Should not make you a non-participant,
Don't be ignorant of the people around you,
Or you may find yourself
In a predicament too,
Lend a helping hand and treat everyone
With compassion and kindness,
For when you shower respect on one and all,
Only then, it truly empowers.
You have made it this far today,
As you know you are the best,
But building yourself and your peers up,
Makes you a cut above the rest.

Krissh Dongre
Watford Grammar School For Boys, Watford

To Everyone

To everyone,
If you want to pass all your dreams,
And you want to succeed,
Then don't make any greed,
And to me, heed.

You must be kind,
And you must find
Happiness,
So you can bind with succession.

You must be loyal,
And love those who love you,
You must not tell lies,
No fibs, tales or untruths.

You must listen,
Talk to people,
Agree or disagree,
If you just concede,
Then you can be who you want to be.

You must have heart,
Not give up,
And even in the hardest of times,
You must not let go,

To what you believe
Is your dream.

Matheesha Gunathilaka (12)
Watford Grammar School For Boys, Watford

Life

From the opening to the close, it is not something to dispose,
The ups and the downs go round and round like a merry-go-round,
It can be cruel, it can be nice, but in the end, it is just a roll of the dice,
It is all about personality, not nationality,
Go for gold for your future to unfold,
Mistakes are good as long as you don't put them under a hood,
Locking them away is still letting them stay,
And to remove you must improve and make the move,
Have to be kind, it's defined by the mind.
Focus on family,
Don't act maliciously,
Make the most of it,
As it's your one shot for success.

Charlie Jenkins (12)
Watford Grammar School For Boys, Watford

Future Me

Future me, I hope for you to see,
That all your dreams are meant to be,
So stop thinking and make it come true,
If anyone will do it, it's gonna be you!

Persevere, it will eventually work,
And if it doesn't, then don't feel hurt!
Don't just sit there, ask for help,
Let out a great big yelp!

You know that Rome wasn't built in one day.
So don't just expect to make your accomplishments today,
Just show resilience and never stop,
You know it, you'll reach the top!

Elias Al-Hindawi (11)
Watford Grammar School For Boys, Watford

Dear Future Me

Dear future me
promise me when days come to rue
there's one man who can get through it
and that one man is you.

Dear future me
when times get crazy
put your mind to it
don't be lazy.

Dear future me
when times get suspicious
stick to your game
just stay ambitious.

Dear future me
just follow your dreams
don't let anyone interfere
with your needs.

Dear future me
just be you
stick to things
you need to do.

Dear future me
don't let anyone
get in your head
stick to being yourself instead.

Diego Pisanu (11)
Watford Grammar School For Boys, Watford

Dear Future Me

Dear future me
I ask you one thing
When you get knocked down
Get back up without a frown

Dear future me
Success won't come first time
But remember where you want to be
Focus and you will be fine

Dear future me
Always believe that you can
And not that you can't
And make those changes to be motivated in life

Dear future me
Never give up
Keep your head up high
Keep motivated
And you will reach for the sky

Dear future me
Every day will be different
Don't lose focus and try new things
Empowerment is what you need
For you to strive.

Danyal Moledina (12)
Watford Grammar School For Boys, Watford

Never Give Up

You have the power to do something
There is no such word as nothing
You have the power to be number one
Don't let this opportunity be gone

Don't let them get the better of you
Confidence is with you too
You will be remembered for what you do
Your life is all about you

Never give up
Do what your heart tells you
Never give up
Your soul will be with you too

Never give up
We always will support you
Never give up
God will be with you too.

Never give up!

Dhruv Datt
Watford Grammar School For Boys, Watford

Empowering

Take me down and I'll rise back up,
Turn me away and I'll rise back up,
I don't care if you say I can't,
I don't care if you think I can't,
I'll come back every time,
Just to show, I'll never give up

Maybe I can't, maybe I can,
All I know is I will try,
Fail or succeed, I've tried;
That's all that matters now,
I can say I've pushed my limits,
I can say I've not given up,
I will make my stand.

Gabriel Elijah Boxall
Watford Grammar School For Boys, Watford

Never Stop

Dear future me,
Right now, I always think it's cheerful,
Whether it's a film or a novel
Never stop loving Marvel

Dear future me
I always think it's clean
I guess it's in my genes
Never stop loving green

Dear future me
I always gotta have it
I always want a bite
Never stop loving pasta

Dear future me
Sometimes I would see them on the balcony
We would play together happily
Never stop loving your family.

Anay Shah (11)
Watford Grammar School For Boys, Watford

Judging

I go to a shop that sells humanity and freedom.
The world wants to put me on a stage,
But all I want to do is stay in my
Lonely cave.
The essence of prosperity and the knowledge of
Charities,
Got to heal the injuries of the past generations.
The mistakes that we make are just a fib of our
Imagination - another examination
If the earth is our oyster
Then where is the judge?
No discrimination, only inspiration.

Eeshan Shah (12)
Watford Grammar School For Boys, Watford

Never Give Up

Never give up,
Keep trying,
Always do your best,
Remember to be kind.

Never give up,
Always be respectful,
Respect others all the time,
Remember to be nice.

Never give up,
Try to help others,
Always be friendly,
Try to talk to others.

Never give up,
Treat others well,
Never be mean,
And remember, look your best.

Shaylan Patel (11)
Watford Grammar School For Boys, Watford

To The Class Of 2021

Filled with strife
This year was hard
We tried to push through
Whilst hiding our scars

Each and every day
Life would become more manic
There's no need to cry
There's no need to panic

To all those who suffered
For all those who cried
You'll never be a disappointment
So don't even try

This year is over
The madness has ended
You can finally relax
Next year will be splendid.

Toby Law (12)
Watford Grammar School For Boys, Watford

My Will

I could
I could try
I could work
I could have fun
I could relax and enjoy my life
I could succeed

I will
I will try
I will work
I will have fun
I will relax and enjoy my life
I will succeed

I have tried
I have worked
I have had fun
I have relaxed and enjoyed my life
I have succeeded.

Luca Shah
Watford Grammar School For Boys, Watford

Dear Future Me

Dear future me,
Always follow your dreams,
Never give up, but try your best,
One small step can finish the rest.

Dear future me,
Always be confident,
Do what you think is right,
Not what others might.

Dear future me,
Always follow your dreams,
And never give up.

Himnish Nandyala
Watford Grammar School For Boys, Watford

YOUNG WRITERS INFORMATION

We hope you have enjoyed reading this book – and that you will continue to in the coming years.

If you're the parent or family member of an enthusiastic poet or story writer, do visit our website **www.youngwriters.co.uk/subscribe** and sign up to receive news, competitions, writing challenges and tips, activities and much, much more! There's lots to keep budding writers motivated!

If you would like to order further copies of this book, or any of our other titles, then please give us a call or order via your online account.

Young Writers
Remus House
Coltsfoot Drive
Peterborough
PE2 9BF
(01733) 890066
info@youngwriters.co.uk

Join in the conversation!
Tips, news, giveaways and much more!